LNER K4 2-6-0 No. 61994 *The Great Marquess* departs from Whitby with the 11am to Goathland on October 23, 2007. BRIAN SHARPE

CONTENTS

THE WORLD'S MOST POPULAR STEAM LINE

MOORS STEAM

NORTH YORKSHIRE MOORS RAILWAY

Author:
Robin Jones

Designer:
Leanne Lawrence

Reprographics:
Jonathan Schofield,
Simon Duncan

Senior sub-editor:
Dan Sharp

Production manager:
Craig Lamb

Marketing manager:
Charlotte Park

Publisher:
Tim Hartley

Commercial director:
Nigel Hole

Publishing director:
Dan Savage

Published by:
Mortons Media Group Ltd,
Media Centre,
Morton Way, Horncastle,
Lincolnshire LN9 6JR
Tel: 01507 529529

Printed by:
William Gibbons and Sons,
Wolverhampton

Credits:
Grateful thanks to NYMR
managing director Philip Benham
and archivist Mark Sissons for
their help in compiling this
publication.

All pictures marked * are published
under a Creative Commons licence.
Full details may be obtained at
http://creativecommons.org/licences

ISBN 978-1-909128-49-1

MORTONS
MEDIA GROUP LTD

Welcome to the North Yorkshire Moors Railway

LNER B1 4-6-0 No. 61264 heads
away from Levisham past Skelton
Tower and into Newtondale on
November 3, 2007. DAVE RODGER

LNER A4 streamlined Pacific No. 60007 *Sir Nigel Gresley* climbs the 1-in-49 gradient away from Beck Hole on October 29, 2006. BRIAN SHARPE

Almost 50 years ago – on March 6, 1965 – the last trains headed out over the moors between Whitby and Pickering. A victim of the infamous Beeching Axe, the railway between Grosmont and Rillington, near Malton was closed, and most people assumed that the old Whitby and Pickering railway, one of the first in England having been opened in 1836, was no more.

However, there were those who thought otherwise and within a few short years not only had a preservation society been formed, but also negotiations were being held with British Railways. In 1973, with vital local authority support, the line reopened between Grosmont and Pickering.

Today the railway is one of Yorkshire's main tourist attractions with a turnover of more than £5 million, generating more than £30 million for the regional economy.

The North Yorkshire Moors Railway carries more passengers than any other heritage railway, not only in the United Kingdom but worldwide.

It is also, so far, the only heritage railway licensed to operate over the national rail network.

In 2013, the NYMR celebrated the 40th anniversary of public services and we are now looking forward to our half century and beyond.

This new history of the line explains how this came about while also covering the development of the railway back from its earliest days. The story is brought right up to date including the extension of services over Network Rail's Esk Valley line and the most recent project to reopen a second platform at Whitby station.

The Whitby and Pickering Railway was designed by no less than the 'Father of Railways' George Stephenson. The first trains were little more than 'stage coaches on wheels', being horse drawn.

In the 1840s, the infamous railway baron George Hudson rescued the railway from near penury setting it on course to become part of the North Eastern Railway which would come to dominate the railway scene in the North of England. For over a century the line from Malton through Pickering to Whitby was a major transport artery with trains to York and West Yorkshire, while in the summer there were even through trains from King's Cross.

Although all this came to an end with the 1965 closure, the resurrection of the line as the North Yorkshire Moors Railway has, if anything, been even more exciting.

From the earliest preservation days it was volunteers who kick-started the reopening project and they remain at the heart of railway's operations, working alongside a core of paid staff. Without them, the NYMR could not possibly survive and I see this publication as a tribute to their dedication and commitment.

**Philip Benham, Managing Director,
North Yorkshire Moors Railway
July 4, 2014**

One of many fabulous works of art produced by the LNER to promote Whitby as a magical destination, which it still very much is today. This poster is part of the National Railway Museum's unrivalled collection in York and can be inspected through its Search Engine library facility, with many of the posters also available as prints or other souvenirs. NRM

THE LINE FOR ALL SEASONS

The North Yorkshire Moors Railway is more than just a preserved steam line. It is a national treasure.

Indeed, it has developed into three attractions in one.

Firstly, it is a showcase for many of Britain's finest historic steam locomotives, several of which are based there, while others arrive or are hired as guests for galas and special occasions. It has seen everything, from humble industrial saddle tanks to mighty LNER Pacifics such as Britain's postwar steam record holder, streamlined A4 No. 60007 *Sir Nigel Gresley*, whose image graces the cover of this publication.

Secondly, it is a unique transport corridor, allowing visitors to experience the best of the North Yorkshire Moors National Park and the wonderfully atmospheric port of Whitby without resorting to the car. Indeed, it is possible to use the line for a week's hiking holiday without the use of rubber wheels.

Thirdly, it is a linear museum. The Grosmont to Pickering line runs through a wealth of remains from the great industrial concerns which once populated the route, giving it a very different character to the one most visitors popularly associate with the line today. The building of the railway by George Stephenson opened up the mineral wealth of the moors, and far from the idyllic vision of purple heather-clad uplands and babbling becks we know and love today, for much of the route's history it ran through a region that had become closer to the Black Country in appearance. There is so much there from the industry of yesteryear if you care to look.

The route has metamorphosed through several eras on its way to becoming a star 'must see' tourism attraction which often carries the best part of 350,000 passengers a year – a figure likely to increase with the opening of a dedicated platform 2 at Whitby in summer 2014.

It started out as wild and windy moors which acted as a natural barrier between Whitby and the rest of England, leaving shipping as the best means of communication with the outside world. Then along came George Stephenson who looked at the line's budget, and despite revolutionising transport with his perfection of the early steam locomotive principle in *Rocket*, opted to build what else but a horse-drawn railway.

Then we had its takeover and conversion to steam by railway magnate George Hudson's empire, in which the railway played its part in the early mass tourist industry during his promotion of Whitby as a mainstream resort. Indeed, much of the shape of the town, particularly the West Cliff area, can be linked to the history of the railway.

Then there were the North Eastern Railway years, during which lineside industries flourished, many of them linked to the railway by their own private sidings or narrow-gauge systems.

After the Grouping of 1923 came the 'Big Four', during which time the LNER experienced success with steam railcars on the route.

Finally came the British Railways era, which paralleled soaring levels of private car ownership and the snowballing closure and eradication of country railways which reached new heights with the appointment of Dr Richard Beeching as chairman. Before the 1964 election, Labour promised to sack him and reverse his cuts, yet once in office, it not only did neither, but also implemented closures over and above those he had recommended. Whitby once had four routes leading into it; it would be left with only the Esk Valley line from Middlesbrough.

Pleas to retain the Whitby to Pickering and Malton route, if only because of the severe winter weather experienced on the top of the moors, fell on deaf ears.

We popularly remember 1967 as the year of flower power and the Summer of Love. Yet while everyone else seemed to be going to San Francisco in mind if not in body, a man called Tom Salmon set about recruiting like-minded people to save a railway which had closed two years before. For him, and what started out as a small band, it was not too late…

Thanks to his vision, the roots of the NYMR were sown that year, but it would be another six before Grosmont to Pickering was reopened throughout as a public railway.

We will forever owe the likes of Tom and his team an immeasurable debt of gratitude. However, thanks must also, in the case of the NYMR, go to the local authorities which not only supported the revivalists but even pushed them to go further. Initially, just Grosmont to

Ellerbeck was considered as a steam heritage line, but North Riding County Council persuaded the volunteer-led preservationists to take a deep breath, close their eyes, and go all the way to Pickering. They never had cause to look back and neither have we.

The same situation arose in the first decade of the 21st century when fears that running scheduled services from the NYMR over a section of the national network into Stephenson's original terminus of Whitby would financially cripple the railway. Fortune again favoured the bold, nobody lost a penny, and look what we have today.

The NYMR is a line for all seasons, not just the peak summer periods. It is an enthralling experience to ride over it in any weather, at any time of the year – when the spring lineside flowers are in bloom, the bucket-and-spade days of July and August, the rich colours of autumn and the snowbound winter times, when the steam train takes the strain far better than any other form of local transport. And that is not to mention the spring and autumn galas and special events such as the line's famous 1940s weekend, all of which go a very long way to filling empty hotel rooms and restaurants out of season.

This book is intended to unfold some of the many and seemingly infinite delights of travelling from Pickering to Whitby, not only as a linear journey but also one through time.

Robin Jones
editor
Heritage Railway

MAIN AND LEFT: A line for all seasons richly prized by railway photographers and passengers alike: NYMR-based Schools class 4-4-0 No. 30926 *Repton* steams past autumn foliage at Beck Hole on October 30, 2003, and runs through Darnholm after a fresh snowfall on December 30, exactly two months later.
PAUL CHANCELOR/BRIAN SHARPE

CHAPTER ONE

REVERSE TECHNOLOGY
The Whitby & Pickering Railway

The insignia of the Whitby & Pickering
Railway. ROBIN JONES

PART of the great charm of red-tile roofed Whitby, one of the real jewels of the coast of north-east England, is its comparative isolation. The moors of Cleveland provide a natural barrier that gives the feeling that the port lying in an enclave at the mouth of the River Esk is all but cut off from the rest of England.

Historically, Whitby was always far easier to reach by sea than by land: indeed, driving over the moors today in the depths of winter can be a daunting task to be avoided wherever possible.

However, Whitby's biggest asset was its coastal position, where a sizeable harbour developed.

The first pier known to have been built in Whitby was the Burgess or Tate Hill pier dating from 1190. In 1632 the Lord of the Manor, Sir Hugh Cholmley, began raising funds for a pier on the west side of the town, and in 1702, an Act of Parliament was granted for the current East and West piers to be built in stone.

Whitby makes no secret about its association with Captain James Cook (1728-1779), the Royal Navy captain, explorer, navigator and cartographer who made the first recorded European contact with the eastern coastline of Australia and the Hawaiian Islands, and the first recorded circumnavigation of New Zealand.

As a teenager, he became apprenticed to Whitby ship owners and Quakers John and Henry Walker, who were in the coal trade. Their house is now the Captain Cook Memorial Museum. A replica of Cook's ship, the *Bark Endeavour Whitby*, offers trips around Whitby harbour throughout the year. However, Whitby's best-known attraction is its ruined clifftop Benedictine abbey, originally founded in AD 657 by Hild with the support of Oswy, ruler of Northumbria. It was the setting in 664 for the Synod of Whitby, at which it was ruled

Map of the original Whitby & Pickering Railway.

PLAN OF WHITBY AND PICKERING RAILWAY.

that the Church would adopt the Roman calculation of Easter, thereby severing ties with the Celtic Christian traditions and meaning that the Pope's authority would prevail in England.

At the time of the abbey's dissolution by Henry VIII in 1539, Whitby had around 30 houses and a population of 200.

At the end of the 16th century, naturalist Thomas Chaloner visited alum works in Italy and saw that the rock being processed was similar to that under his Guisborough estate. Alum was important for medicinal uses, curing leather and as a dye fixative and had previously been imported from Spain and Italy, but after England's break with Rome the supply had been cut off. Chaloner secretly brought in workmen to develop the industry in Yorkshire, and alum quarries were set up along the Yorkshire coast.

After the alum industry had been established Whitby benefited enormously as a port and the town branched out into shipbuilding. Cook's *HMBark Endeavour* was originally built in the town in 1764 as a coal collier called *Earl of Pembroke* before later refitting in Deptford, and other vessels were built for the Newcastle to London coal trade. By 1795 Whitby had become

a major whaling port with whalebone being the plastic of its day and the oil used for lighting and lubrication.

During Georgian times, Whitby prospered and the town's existing Georgian buildings were built during this time by wealthy ship owners and builders. However, by the 1820s, the industries of Whitby were in marked long-term decline, with whaling and shipbuilding no longer bringing in the revenue they once did. Despite its many successes as a port, Whitby suffered from poor land communications, which mainly comprised only bridleways and flagged causeways.

The statue of Captain Cook overlooking Whitby harbour. ROBIN JONES

A contemporary painting of a horse-drawn Whitby & Pickering Railway coach at the Tunnel Inn. WHITBY MUSEUM

A turnpike road which opened from Pickering in 1759 still involved a long haul over the moors of North Yorkshire.

An early form of stagecoach known as a diligence began running from York to Whitby in 1788, but fully fledged stagecoach services to Whitby did not start for another seven years and mail coaches did not run to the port until 1823. In winter such journeys were uncomfortable and potentially dangerous.

Then there was also a problem of bulk carriages of goods over the uplands to the North Yorkshire port. In 1793, the idea of a canal from Whitby to Pickering was mooted, but it came to nothing, as the moorland terrain was considered impracticable for such an undertaking.

THE LURE OF THE IRON HORSE

Three decades later, Whitby businessmen looked northwards to Stockton-on-Tees, the southern terminus of the world's first public steam-hauled railway, the Stockton & Darlington, when it opened on September 27, 1825, engineered by the brilliant one-time illiterate colliery hand and self-taught engineer George Stephenson.

Indeed, as early as 1818, 19 leading Whitby townsfolk had subscribed to the Stockton & Darlington Railway, presumably out of desperation for better land transport links for their port. In 1826, the Whitby and Pickering Turnpike Road Act came up for renewal, and serious questions were again posed about land transport.

An article from a contributor called Amicus appeared in the *Whitby Repository* in September that year, calling for a railway to be built, and appeared to sum up the widely held view of the town's residents and traders.

Amicus wrote: "This proposed alteration (of the road) also favours and may in the end be the means of promoting another plan, which I trust will at some future time occupy the attention of the town and neighbourhood.

"It may be thought completely chimerical at present, though I am very sanguine in my ideas and expectations that it will take place at some time or other; I mean a railway from Whitby across the moors to the interior of the country, by the way of Pickering.

TO CONTRACTORS.

THE Directors of the WHITBY and PICKERING RAILWAY, are ready to Contract for the Execution of the whole of the Works on the remaining 8¼ Miles of the Whitby and Pickering Railway. Plans, Sections, Drawings, and Specifications, may be seen at the RAILWAY-OFFICE, WHITBY, between the 7th and 29th Iust., after which date, no Tenders will be received.
By Order of the Directors,
GEO. STEPHENSON, Engineer.

The invitation to tender for constructing the final 8½ miles of the Whitby & Pickering Railway.

Crossing the North Yorkshire Moors in the depths of winter can be a daunting prospect even with today's surfaced roads, so imagine what it would have been like when bridleways were the only route. ROBIN JONES

A contemporary drawing of a Whitby & Pickering Railway service.

The Whitby weigh houses as depicted in Illustrations of the scenery of the line of the Whitby & Pickering Railway by Henry Belcher in 1836.

"Situated as we are, the only convenient seaport between the Tees and Humber, and with a rich and fertile country completely available to us at a distance of only 20 miles; let us not sit down in sullen lethargy and consider ourselves and the good town we live in of so little importance as not to be worth a thought. If we do, we deceive ourselves and suffer other towns less favourably situated and possessing not half the advantages we do to emerge from that insignificance which nature intended them, and by the public spirit of their native sons rise into an importance they were never designed to possess; nay rival, and even supersede, us by those energies which in us are latent and which, if aroused and exercised, will prevent their forming even an idea which in competition with us would be futile and useless.

"The continental trade, since the peace (end of the Napoleonic Wars), has been and is still likely to be carried on to a very great extent. All the country from Pickering to Scarborough, Malton, Kirby-Moorside, Helmsley, the Dales &c. is supplied with every article of importation either from Scarborough or Hull, but chiefly from the latter place; whereas if a railway was made from Whitby to Pickering, all this trade, or nearly so, would fall into our hands. For this natural reason – we could

The Angel Hotel opposite Whitby station, where George Stephenson's recommendation for the route of the railway from Pickering was accepted at a meeting on September 12, 1832.
ROBIN JONES

The replica of Captain Cook's *HMB Endeavour* enters Whitby harbour. ROBIN JONES

undersell both these places considerably.

"If there was a railway from Whitby to Pickering, and from thence to Malton, Baltic produce of every description could be delivered there for nearly 20s a ton less than it can possibly be from Hull; besides the greater facility in point of time, water carriage being slow and tedious and liable, for three months in the winter, to be impeded or stopped altogether.

"The railway should go in a parallel line with the proposed Turnpike Road, and there is not the least doubt if it could be established but it would prove a most advantageous speculation.

"Upwards of 30 years ago a navigable communication between Whitby and Pickering was in agitation. An eminent engineer, Mr Crosley, was employed to accurately survey, measure and take the levels on the intermediate ground. The line of the canal was laid down from Whitby, parallel with the river Esk, to Growmond Bridge, from thence by Hunt House in Goathland to Fensteps, near the present Pickering road at Ellerbeck Bridge, and from thence down Newton Dale to Pickering, making the whole distance about 25 miles. The canal was to have been 4½ft deep, 30ft wide at the top and 18ft wide at the bottom, such dimensions being sufficient to allow barges of 25 tons burthen to pass each other. The size of each lock was to have been 24 yards long, four yards wide and four yards deep, containing 384 cubic yards each.

"The nearest calculation of the time of passing from one place to the other was upwards of 18 hours, under the most favourable circumstances; but it would, no doubt, have been a much longer time, whereas by a railway, which would not be more than 19 miles, it would not take one-fourth of the time. The expense of the proposed canal was estimated at £66,447. Even at that time when there was a great stagnation of trade… the returns arising from an estimate of the tonnage that was likely to be conveyed thereon… were pronounced in the report of the committee at that period; not only to be sufficient to pay the annual sum of £1652 18s 4d for agencies, repairs and other contingent expenses, but to leave also a clear interest of 5% to the subscribers. What ought we now to expect to realize from a railway which would not cost perhaps half the money, and the annual

A horse-drawn train passes the cutting at Eskdale, as seen in a G Dodgson sketch published in 1836.

Incline Cottage stands at the foot of George Stephenson's rope-hauled incline at Beck Hole on the original Whitby & Pickering Railway route. The incline was abandoned in 1864 in favour of the current deviation through today's Goathland station. The building is thought to have been used as a booking office. BRIAN SHARPE

expense and charges of which would not be one-third of the above sum?

"To meet the expenses &c, we possess the advantages which they at that time could not possibly calculate on; the continental trade being now carried on to a great extent. All the Baltic produce, as I have before stated, would be sent to those places from Whitby. All their goods from London would be shipped for Whitby and transmitted from thence by the railway to their respective purchasers."

In 1830, many shipyards had by this time closed or were on the brink, and the alum works were gone. Local businessmen, including Robert Campion, made serious enquiries about the possibility of building a railway from Whitby to Pickering.

The two years that followed saw much deliberation about whether a railway should be built, and if so whether it should run to Stockton and join the Stockton & Darlington, or south to Pickering.

Campion initially favoured Stockton and the route was actually surveyed by Thomas Storey, who reported on March 2, 1831, on two options. This led to a committee being set up to fund a proper survey by Storey. Doubts subsequently set in, especially when Storey later 'modified' his estimate to twice the cost!

A FUTURE IN THE PAST

In the early summer of 1832, George Stephenson himself was asked to give his opinion.

He came down on the side of the Pickering option. He pointed out that the Stockton & Darlington already had a port in Middlesbrough, and there was no advantage to traders in paying for a rail journey eastwards to Whitby just to use the harbour.

However, he argued, a line running south to Pickering could carry both cheap coal to towns and villages in North Yorkshire and fertiliser, which would allow large barren tracts of moorland to be cultivated.

"The revenue arising from the use of the Whitby & Pickering Railway will amply remunerate the proprietors for the money invested," Stephenson wrote.

However, the man whose name is immortalised by its link with *Rocket*, the engine he and his son Robert built to win the Rainhill Trials of 1829 and run on the world's first inter-city railway, the Liverpool & Manchester, went on to make a recommendation that seems astonishing to modern readers.

While *Rocket* is regarded as the first 'modern' steam engine, and the Rainhill Trials finally ended the debate as to whether horses or steam locomotives were the future of transport, Stephenson recommended that the

A contemporary sketch of a horse train crossing Fen Bog near Newtowndale.

proposed Whitby to Pickering Railway should use horses.

Twenty years after Stephenson had built his first steam engine, *Blücher*, and three decades after Richard Trevithick unveiled his first self-propelled steam vehicles, the great

railway engineer wanted the clock to be turned back. To us, it might seem like Microsoft's Bill Gates reverting to sliderules or even an abacus.

However, Stephenson was made aware that the line had nothing like the budget for the

The bridge over the River Esk at Ruswarp.

A pastoral scene of 1836 from the southern part of the line. G DODGSON

Twin arches which once carried the Whitby & Pickering Railway over the Murk Esk. PAULINE E*

View up the incline, now a popular public footpath between Moorgates and Goathland. Hemp rope was wound around a wooden drum and water tanks used as a counterbalance, allowing the carriages to be hauled up the inclined plane. PAULINE E*

The route of the original railway south of Goathland. KA*

Liverpool & Manchester, and knew that over the moors of North Yorkshire the cloth would have to be cut accordingly, and by comparison drastically.

Stephenson's recommendation was accepted at a meeting held at the Angel Inn in Whitby on September 12, 1832.

A share list was immediately opened and £30,000 was subscribed to it there and then; the estimated total cost of building the 26 mile line being £80,000, and Stephenson was appointed engineer.

The Whitby & Pickering Railway Bill received Royal Assent from William IV on May 6, 1833.

By August that year, contracts for building the first section, from Bog Hall in Whitby to Sleights, was let and the first sod was dug by local businessman Robert Campion.

Again, Stephenson was under no illusions; the modest budget had to be adhered to, so there would be no world firsts like the building of the magnificent nine-arch Sankey Viaduct.

Instead, rather than move mountains, he engineered a 1500 yard-long rope-worked incline at an average gradient of 1-in-15 to take the line up from the valley of the Murk Esk at Beck Hole to the high moors at Goathland, rather than build an expensive and winding route to climb the hills gradually.

Stephenson's line also crossed Fen Bog, near the summit of the line, using the same techniques he famously employed on the Liverpool & Manchester at Chat Moss, here using a bed of timber and with moorland heather bound in sheep fleece to float the railway over the mire.

Promoters hoped to link the railway to York, and in September 1834, a meeting to that purpose was held in the city. It was there that George Stephenson may have met the man who would later become known as the Railway King, George Hudson.

THE RAILWAY OPENS

The first section of the Whitby & Pickering Railway was opened between Whitby and the Tunnel Inn at Grosmont on Monday, June 8, 1835.

The railway had been promoted for carrying freight including coal, stone, timber and limestone, but it was also intended to run passenger trains from the start. Three first-class stagecoach-type vehicles adapted for railway use, *Premier*, *Transit* and *Lady Hilda*, were obtained, the first from Beeston & Melling of Manchester, along with some other cheaper locally built vehicles.

In July 1835, the railway ran a coach between Whitby and Ruswarp for the Ruswarp Fair. It ended up becoming a centrepiece of the event itself, with several passengers making more than one journey just for the ride.

It cost £105,000 to build the railway which opened as a single-track line throughout on May 26, 1836, the track consisting of wrought-iron fish-bellied rails in 15ft lengths. It remained horse worked for its entire independent life.

The ceremonial opening saw policemen stationed throughout the length of the line to deal with incidents of drunkenness and

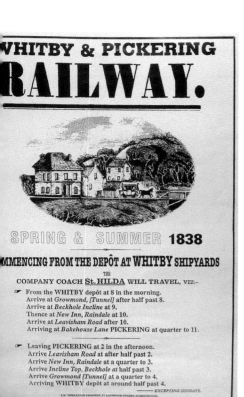

A section of George Stephenson's original Whitby & Pickering Railway track, with the rails fastened to stone blocks, re-created at Pickering station. ROBIN JONES

disorderly behaviour.

The day started with glorious sunshine, with church bells in Whitby ringing and crowds gathering outside the Angel Inn at 7.30am, where the Whitby Brass Band played.

Campion, the chairman, and the directors walked from there to the railway depot, where their procession was received with three cheers.

A bell rang and the horses were attached to the carriages, immediately starting off towards Pickering, with crowds lining either side of the railway. Every vantage point was crowded with spectators.

Arriving at the Tunnel Inn, visitors saw lime kilns being built by the Whitby and Grosmond Lime Company, one of several concerns founded to take advantage of the railway.

The passengers were also shown the Whitby

Stone Company's rail-connected quarry at Lease Rigg, with its self-acting inclined plane.

The passenger train ascended the main line's incline with ease. When the downward gradient began, the horses were detached and the carriages allowed to run down on their own at speeds of up to 30mph, with the guard's steady hand on the brakes.

After the coupled carriages came to rest, a team of fresh horses took the train onwards to Pickering, where the hill on which the town's medieval castle stands was covered with spectators.

From the station, the Pickering town band and others from neighbouring towns, including Scarborough, led a procession to the Black Swan Inn, where a dinner was laid on for the VIP party.

In his book, Illustrations of the scenery on the line of the Whitby and Pickering railway in the north eastern part of Yorkshire, published that year, Henry Belcher wrote: "Justly celebrated as is the name of Stephenson for the

astonishing perfection to which he has advanced the art of travelling on railways by means of locomotive engines; yet the peculiar character of the country through which the Whitby and Pickering Railway had to be formed, and the limited means of the company imposed upon him and Mr Swanwick his able assistant, a necessity to forego, in some degree, an adherence to those rules (more particularly as to curves and gradients) which necessarily guide an engineer in the laying out and construction of great public lines of railway.

"It should, in justice to all parties, be distinctly borne in mind not only that there were many formidable natural difficulties in the making a railway from Whitby to Pickering, but that the district being comparatively unknown to the public, and the prospect of traffic and remuneration being of a nature not likely to be satisfactory except to persons residing in the neighbourhood, and fully aware of its natural and artificial resources and of the probable effect of calling those resources into

action by means of a railway, the expense of the undertaking had to be borne almost exclusively by the inhabitants of Whitby and Pickering and their immediate friends. And that therefore, unless a railway could be constructed for an amount which it was calculated would be the utmost extent that they could raise, the prospect of procuring one at all must have been abandoned.

"Such were, in fact, the instructions given to the engineer, who therefore entered upon his important duties under every circumstance of disadvantage: for instead of having a more than usual supply of means for forming a railway through a district full of natural impediments, and consequently requiring a more than ordinary command of money, he was obliged to contrive such a railway as could, by possibility, be constructed for the given sum to which the promoters of the undertaking confined him.

"Notwithstanding all these difficulties, the survey was made, an estimate formed, an act applied for and obtained, the railway commenced, and, in three years from the passing of the act, completed; and all at an expense that makes the average cost amount to no more than about $4400 a mile."

In its first year of operation, the railway carried 10,000 tonnes of stone from Grosmont to Whitby, as well as 6000 passengers, who paid a fare of one shilling to sit on the roof of a coach or one shilling and three pence to sit inside. It took two and a half hours to travel from Whitby to Pickering.

The railway ran a regular passenger service linking at Pickering with the stagecoach to York, which by then was rail connected.

While stagecoaches were superseded by steam railways, for some time they opened up fresh opportunities for services to link railways to outlying places yet to be reached by branch lines.

Heavy snowfalls at the end of 1836 showed the wisdom of building the railway. Roads were impassable, the mail could not get through and Whitby would have been cut off – save for the railway, which continued running to its timetable.

The original bridge over the River Esk in Eskdale. G DODGSON

Right: A plaque at Whitby station marking the 150th anniversary of George Stephenson's line. ROBIN JONES

Below: The Whitby & Pickering Railway weigh station built on the original Stephenson line half a mile west of the current Whitby station and taken from a North Yorkshire Moors Railway train. PHILIP BENHAM

An advertisement for services on the new railway.

STEAM MAKES ITS DEBUT

The Whitby & Pickering Railway became part of George Hudson's York & North Midland Railway in 1845 when he bought it for £80,000. A bill authorising the sale and which received royal assent on June 30 that year permitted the introduction of steam locomotives.

It was then rebuilt on an amended but broadly similar route as a double-track steam-worked railway, with new stations along the line, most of which survive today. The first steam train service between Pickering and Levisham ran on September 1, 1846, and the rebuilt line was opened in stages until it was completed throughout on July 1, 1847.

The first steam locomotive, a 2-2-0, had entered Whitby on June 4, driven by Edward Laws, with its fireman the aptly named William Pickering.

The line was extended southwards to meet the York & North Midland's York to Scarborough line at Rillington Junction near Malton, which opened on July 7, 1845. The first passenger services between Rillington and Pickering were running by October.

Other locomotives which ran to Whitby in the early days of the line's new steam era included two 0-4-0s, *Firefly* and *Greyhound*.

The new connection afforded Whitby rail access to the industrial north, eventually

Above: One of the most significant features on Stephenson's original Whitby & Pickering Railway was this 130 yard tunnel cut through rock at Grosmont. Designed by Stephenson's assistant Frederick Swanwick, then just 22, it is believed to be one of the oldest railway tunnels in the world. Swanwick was rebuked by the directors for wasting money on this castellated portal at the north end at a time when the railway company was trying to keep expenditure to the bare minimum. It is now used as public footpath to access Grosmont locomotive works. ROBIN JONES

bringing in day trippers and holidaymakers, along with the morning mail train, while sounding the final death knell for stagecoaches.

In 1854, the York & North Midland became part of the North Eastern Railway.

Stephenson's incline at Beck Hole was the scene of a fatal accident in 1864 when the rope snapped.

A four-and-a-half mile diversion to the new Goathland station, avoiding the need for an incline, was by then under construction. Authorised by a Parliamentary Bill of July 11, 1861, it cost £56,000. to build. Once the deviation opened, the route was worked by steam locomotives throughout. ∎

Rocket inventor George Stephenson went back to the days before the steam age to provide traction for his Whitby & Pickering Railway in the form of horses.

CHAPTER 2

GEORGE HUDSON AND WHITBY

MUCH of the popularity of Whitby as a significant holiday destination was down to George Hudson.

As we have seen, his conversion of George Stephenson's horse-drawn railway to a 'modern' steam line brought in the tourists.

All the time, Hudson, the great entrepreneur, was thinking outside the box and was investing big money in ways of keeping them there.

He formed a company to develop Whitby's West Cliff area with roads and hotels, intending to make it a fashionable resort.

He built the Royal Hotel overlooking the harbour entrance along with several boarding houses after laying out streets on West Cliff.

He also cut the winding road called the Khyber Pass into the side of the cliff to allow easy access between his clifftop development and the harbour, especially for the transportation of building materials.

Looking out to sea was the Royal Crescent development, which echoed the grandiose Regency style of houses in places like Bath, Cheltenham and Harrogate.

However, only half of it was ever built because his company ran out of money for reasons we will see below.

Hudson, whose name is recalled in Hudson Street, seems to have had his eye on Whitby as least since 1834, when he met George Stephenson in the port.

While Stephenson has been called the Father of Railways, Hudson became known as the Railway King. However, while the former is credited with shaping so much of the modern world, historians have been left debating whether the latter was a hero – or a villain.

THE FRAUDSTER WHO FELL FROM GRACE

Hudson was born to parents John and Elizabeth Hudson on March 10, 1800. Both of his parents had died by the time he was eight and at 15 he became an apprentice draper for Bell and Nicholson in York.

At the age of 21, he married Nicholson's

George Hudson, the Railway King.
ROBIN JONES COLLECTION

daughter Elizabeth and helped build up the business so that by 1827 it was the biggest of its kind in York. His great-uncle Matthew Botrill later left him a £30,000 fortune… which led him to invest in railways.

He helped to establish the York Union Banking Company which drew up plans for a railway linking the city to Leeds. Hudson subscribed for 500 shares in the scheme and became the largest shareholder, but interest waned after engineer John Rennie produced a blueprint for a horse-drawn affair just like the Whitby & Pickering, and the line was never built.

In 1835, Hudson formed a committee to promote the York & North Midland Railway, which received its Act of Parliament in 1836 and he became its chairman.

The line would join the North Midland Railway, in which Hudson also bought shares, at Normanton. Hudson became chairman of the North Midland in 1842, and held the same position with the Newcastle & Darlington Junction Railway formed that year, and which expanded into the York, Newcastle & Berwick Railway in 1847.

Destructive competition between the Midland Counties Railway, the North Midland Railway and the Birmingham & Derby Junction Railway led to a merger between all three being manoeuvred by Hudson in 1844.

With George Stephenson, Hudson planned an extension to the York & North Midland Railway to Darlington and Newcastle. He convinced Stephenson to route what became today's East Coast Main Line from Newcastle to London through York rather than bypassing the city on the way to Leeds.

The Eastern Counties Railway then extended his empire into East Anglia. By 1844, he

George Hudson's Royal Crescent overlooking the North Sea at Whitby. The Railway King George Hudson aimed to emulate Bath in order to generate a similar tourist trade and commissioned a builder named Langdale to build a Regency crescent and street houses on his West Cliff estate. Only half of the crescent was ever built, because his company ran out of money to complete it. ROBIN JONES

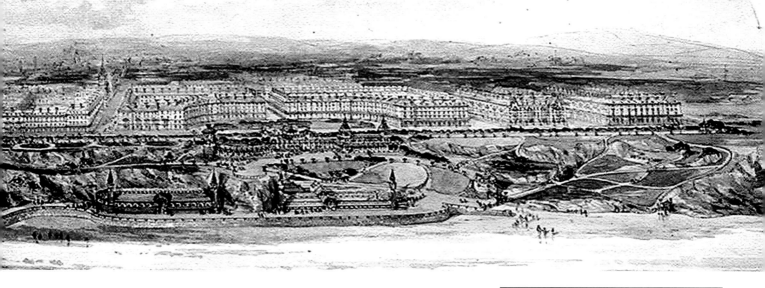

controlled more than 1000 miles of railway.

He expanded and consolidated his companies with tireless energy, unfailing foresight and unbroken success. Because of his sound judgment the lines of his companies were built more cheaply than those of rival companies in the same localities. In 1848 he was at the height of his success.

This was the height of the 'Railway Mania' in which speculators rushed to buy shares in virtually any new scheme which appeared in Britain. English wit, writer and Anglican cleric Sydney Smith coined the term Railway King to describe Hudson.

Hudson became Deputy Lieutenant for Durham, Lord Mayor of York in 1837,1838 and 1846, and Conservative MP for Sunderland from 1845-59.

To mark the coronation of Queen Victoria on June 28, 1838, Hudson treated York's poor parishioners to "an excellent and substantial breakfast" while giving free grocery tickets to 14,000 of the 'lower orders', paid for by public subscription.

While Hudson's steam railway empire boomed, the same could not be said for the Whitby & Pickering Railway. Despite its usefulness, revenue failed to reach even 50% of the level predicted by the line's original

Above: An artist's impression of the massive Regency-style estate which 'Railway King' George Hudson planned to build on the green fields at Whitby West Cliff. Although only a small part was built, the introduction of steam trains by Hudson's York & North Midland Railway after 1845 contributed enormously to the port's popularity as a holiday and day-trip destination, and soon most of the site was built on by other speculators. NYMR ARCHIVES

promoters, and the directors began looking for a way out in the form of a merger or takeover.

With Hudson's plans for his York & North Midland Railway line to Scarborough and its branch to Pickering well advanced, they looked in that direction.

Hudson agreed a purchase price of £80,000, which was £25,000 less than the construction costs borne by the shareholders, who in addition had to find another £30,000 capital afterwards. The sale went through in 1845, heralding a new dawn in the line's infrastructure and its fortunes.

In 1846, Hudson outlined plans for 32 Parliamentary Bills for new railway projects costing a total of £10 million. By then, Hudson's companies controlled over a quarter of the railways then built in England.

George Hudson's Royal Hotel, viewed through the town's whalebone arch. The original bones, donated by a Norwegian firm, were replaced in the 1990s. In 2002 the council acquired new bones from Whitby's twin town in Alaska. They are from a bowhead whale which was killed legally by native Inuit. ROBIN JONES

This pedestrian tunnel in the side of Railway King George Hudson's Khyber Pass smacks of railway architectural influence. ROBIN JONES

The twisting road known as the Khyber Pass, named after a strategic pass in the Afghan wars, allows traffic from Whitby's harbour to climb up to West Cliff, where the green clifftop fields were being developed by George Hudson into a holiday resort. ROBIN JONES

COOKING THE BOOKS

Many honours and rewards were bestowed on Hudson, who was widely acclaimed as a shining example of the new breed of entrepreneur produced in a wave of mid-19th century prosperity.

He became a man of enormous influence and power, but all was not as it seemed. Suddenly, the great bubble burst.

Rumours grew that some of his financial transactions would not stand up to close scrutiny and committees of inquiry were set up.

After the Eastern Counties Railway's share prices declined in value in 1847, he was found to have falsified the books of the Eastern Counties and was exposed as a fraudster.

His sharp business practices – including the paying of shareholders' dividends from company capital and appropriating large sums of money for his personal use – were exposed.

The term 'cooking the books' was first used to refer to George Hudson and has since been immortalised in the English language.

The scandal sent shockwaves throughout Suffolk, which was dependent on the links via the Eastern Counties to London and nationwide.

In early 1849, Eastern Counties Railway shareholders met and forcibly ended Hudson's links with the company.

His status collapsed overnight after he was forced to resign his directorships of all companies he had been involved with. His activities left many shareholders facing ruin, as his shares fell sharply. He brought the Railway Mania period to a swift and painful end.

Furthermore, Hudson was found to have bribed MPs in order to prevent government regulation of railways, but he could do nothing to prevent a committee of investigation being set up to investigate his affairs.

The Committee of Investigation exposed huge scandals created by the business dealings of Hudson, who agreed to pay back the shareholders of the Great North Railway and the Newcastle & Berwick Railway.

The committee looked into the purchase of the Whitby & Pickering Railway – and far from finding that Hudson had swindled anybody, was horrified by the belief he had paid too much.

While Hudson handed over £80,000, the committee found that the line had been worth more like £30,000 at the time, regardless of how much it cost to build. The report from the committee stated: "Your committee cannot sufficiently condemn the most improvident bargain and the unjustified defence in the subsequent outlay." While everywhere else Hudson was being 'outed' as a swindler, here he was painted a fool who had paid over the odds.

In 1849, Hudson was expelled from York City Council and the city's George Hudson Street was renamed Railway Street. The city

Widely reviled when he fell from grace in 1849, George Hudson's bust is now displayed inside the National Railway Museum at York. ROBIN JONES

fathers saw fit to distance themselves from him, much as in modern times people have rushed to erase links with celebrities who have fallen from grace following convictions for criminal offences or allegations thereof. Incidentally, the street regained its original name in 1971.

By the year 1850, his influence upon the railway sector had vanished.

Left broke, Hudson went to France to escape his debts but returned in 1865 with the aim of fighting for the seat at Whitby in the general election that year.

Just before the election, Hudson was arrested for debts and imprisoned at York Castle, where he remained for three months.

He was freed and his remaining friends and admirers raised enough money to pay him a yearly income of £600, allowing him to live with his wife in a small house in London.

Hudson was taken ill in York in the December of 1871 and returned to London, where he died at home. His coffin was taken by train to York and he was buried at Scrayingham, close to his birthplace.

The former millionaire died leaving behind effects worth less than £200.

Scottish philosopher, satirical writer, essayist, historian and teacher Thomas Carlyle condemned Hudson as the "big swollen gambler", but Prime Minister William Gladstone said: "It is a great mistake to look back upon him as a speculator; he was a man of great discernment possessing a great deal of courage and rich enterprise – a very bold and not at all an unwise projector."

Whether he was a hero or a villain is a matter for endless debate. Yes, he was a fraudster, but at the same time, he was a man of wide vision and immense energy who held an honest faith in his schemes.

Hudson challenged the iron grip of the landed gentry and created a huge slice of the national network that we have today. And he yanked the technologically backward railway from Whitby to Pickering into the modern age.

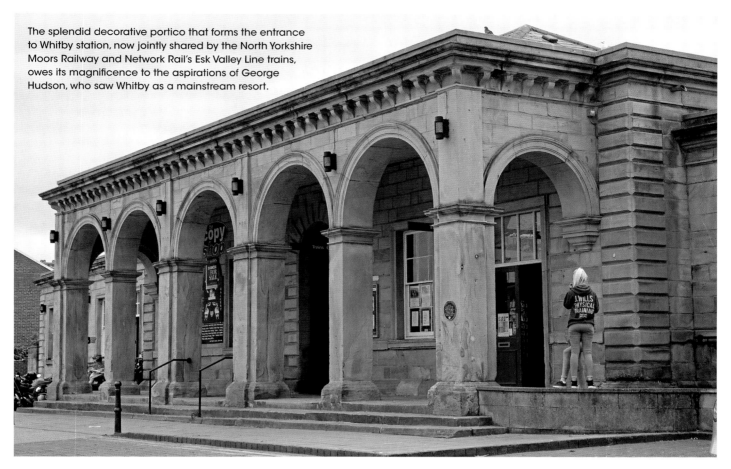

The splendid decorative portico that forms the entrance to Whitby station, now jointly shared by the North Yorkshire Moors Railway and Network Rail's Esk Valley Line trains, owes its magnificence to the aspirations of George Hudson, who saw Whitby as a mainstream resort.

WHITBY'S NEW STATION

Whitby station on George Stephenson's original line stood near to the end of the current platform, containing its offices, workshop and carriage shed.

When Hudson's York & North Midland Railway upgraded the line following its purchase in 1845, converting it to double track and adding steam infrastructure, the existing station was built to the design of Exeter-born YNMR architect George Townsend Andrews (1804–1855) who also designed the locomotive shed and the goods shed.

The new station was built on a curve and comprised two platforms enclosed within stone flanking walls. It was squeezed into a tight area of land adjacent to Dry Dock.

Andrews made his name designing buildings for Hudson's railway empire, especially the YNMR.

He designed all the buildings for the Newcastle & Darlington Junction Railway and the Yorkshire buildings of the York, Newcastle and Berwick Railway.

Amongst his greatest achievements was the first proper York station, which was built for joint use by the YNMR and the Great North of England Railway. It brought the railway into the city for the first time with the lines passing through a new bridge arch in the city walls; previously, the YMR terminated just outside the city walls when it opened in May 1839.

The new York station was laid out to a plan by Robert Stephenson and was an adaptation of his plan for Euston station making allowances for York's status as a junction.

Andrews designed twin trainsheds, each with a 40ft span, and joined at each end,

which produced a hipped appearance, one of Andrews' trademarks. The YNMR boardroom and offices were on the first floor.

Andrews' York station opened on January 4, 1841, and although replaced by the present station in 1877, it remained in use for parcels and carriage stabling until 1966.

His Whitby station also included an example of his 'Euston Truss' overall roof (removed by British Railways in 1953 and replaced by the present awnings). The main building's superb five-bay arcaded decorative portico was demanded by Hudson as part of his strategy to promote Whitby as a resort.

The new Whitby station opened in 1847. With an increase in traffic in the mid-1860s, two bay platforms were provided to the east side of the line.

Andrews also designed headquarters for two York banks and several churches. ■

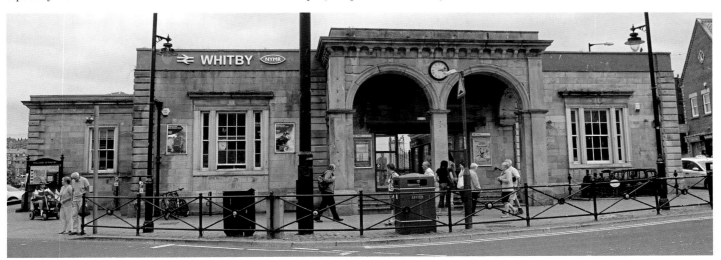

A side view of Whitby station today also highlighting the design of George Townsend Andrews. ROBIN JONES

CHAPTER 3

THE NORTH EASTERN RAILWAY ERA

The NER's first locomotive superintendent Edward Fletcher, who was inherited from the York & North Midland Railway, designed the Cables Class 492 4-4-0s specifically for the Whitby to Pickering line when it opened to locomotive haulage throughout after the Goathland deviation opened in 1865. This example, rebuilt with a cab as No. 1809, is pictured with its crew at Whitby in 1893. The type, which also ran on the Esk Valley line to Stockton-on-Tees, was also known as 'Whitby bogies'. B MASHITER/PENDRAGON COLLECTION

The fall of George Hudson led to declines in the fortunes of railway companies in his empire.

Both the York & North Midland and the York, Newcastle & Berwick railways had to reduce dividends, and future capital expenditure and the building of many authorised lines were suspended.

At the same time, the Leeds Northern Railway opened in 1849, followed by the Great Northern Railway's main line from London to Peterborough the following year.

The GNR and the York & North Midland agreed to bring traffic into York over the latter from Knottingley, superseding the through route to the North from Euston via the York & North Midland and York, Newcastle & Berwick railways.

That upset the Midland Railway and its ally the Manchester, Sheffield & Lincolnshire Railway (later the Great Central), which decided to try to break the new stranglehold that this arrangement created.

The pair diverted all its traffic to the north over the Leeds Northern line.

The YNMR and the York, Newcastle & Berwick companies, which had worked together since being part of the Hudson empire, started a price war in a bid to keep traffic on their old route. York, Newcastle & Berwick tickets for a return 238 mile trip from Leeds to Newcastle in 1852 were cut to two shillings, with slender if any profit margins.

It was clear that financial suicide was in the offing, and so the York, Newcastle & Berwick and Leeds Northern railways began discussing pooling of receipts. Yet they could not leave

out the NYMR because the other two ran their northern traffic over its lines.

The simple solution was to amalgamate. That was no surprise, for most early railway companies were by then joining forces; the three themselves had been formed from 20 smaller companies over the previous two decades.

Following protracted negotiations, on July 31, 1854, the three became the North Eastern Railway.

The new company found itself with more than 700 miles of railway, a higher figure than that of any other company in the UK.

Further amalgamations and the construction of new lines led to its route mileage increasing to 1754, and it became the biggest dock owning railway company in the country, owning 44 acres of harbour.

The area covered by the NER was a triangle drawn between Berwick, Leeds and Spurn Head, inside which the only serious contender was the Stockton & Darlington Railway.

During its first 10 years, the NER continued to expand and consolidate by building new lines and absorbing other companies operating in the district. Its great rival, the Stockton & Darlington, amalgamated with the NER in 1863, allowing the latter to claim direct descent from George Stephenson.

THE WHITBY AND PICKERING NETWORK DEVELOPS

Under the NER, the Whitby to Pickering line became part of a network serving valleys in and around the moors and also the coast to the north and south.

Whitby's second rail connection came via the section of Stephenson's original line from Grosmont.

What is now known as the Esk Valley line – and was the only one left serving the town after the Beeching cuts – is a composite of four separate older routes.

The North Yorkshire & Cleveland Railway built a line from the Northallerton-Eaglescliffe route at Picton eastwards in stages, opening it for mineral traffic as far as Battersby on April 6, 1858, the year in which the company was absorbed into the NER, and to passengers between Stokesley and Castleton on April 1, 1861.

The section between Grosmont and Castleton was the last to be opened, on October 2, 1865.

A line was built from Battersby to

Above: A Whitby to Saltburn service in full flight passes Sandsend, as depicted in a LNER promotional poster. NRM

Right: The viaduct carrying the Whitby to Loftus railway through Sandsend, a small offshoot of a resort that grew up at the northern end of Whitby's sweep of golden sands. BRITISH RAILWAYS

The building of the great Larpool viaduct at Whitby. KEN HOOLE STUDY CENTRE

Whitby as seen from Larpool viaduct in 1910. Note the Whitby & Pickering Railway weight house bottom left. NYMR ARCHIVES

Nunthorpe in 1864, linking it to the Middlesbrough to Guisborough line, which in turn had been constructed by the Middlesbrough & Guisborough Railway in 1854. It is this section that survives in use today as the eastern end of the Esk Valley line, the original route west of Battersby being closed in 1954.

At first, Battersby was known as Ingleby junction, opening when the Ingleby mining company's private line first linked to the North Yorkshire & Cleveland Railway. The station was renamed Battersby Junction in 1878 to avoid confusion with Ingleby station, built nearby on the Rosedale freight-only branch, which ran from Battersby 11 miles across the moors to reach iron ore deposits in the Rosedale valley.

The station became simply Battersby in 1893. By then it had become an important junction, despite being located on single-track routes, with vast loads of ironstone from Rosedale, Glaisdale and Grosmont passing through to feed the blast furnaces of Teesside.

The station became a major hub with extensive marshalling sidings and three-road engine shed with a turntable.

To accommodate the army of railway staff needed to man the station, two terraces with 30 cottages and two other houses were built

and still stand today. Battersby once had three platforms – two lengthy Up and Down line platforms connected by a central footbridge, along with a shorter bay platform with a run-round loop. Water towers were located at both ends of the station.

NORTH OF WHITBY
From what has in past times been known as Whitby Town station, a single track branched up a steep incline to Prospect Hill Junction from which trains could reach Whitby West Cliff station.

From there, trains ran along the coast to Saltburn-by-the-Sea and on to Middlesbrough via the Whitby Redcar and Middlesbrough Union Railway.

The line from Whitby to Loftus, where it joined the NER Middlesbrough-Loftus route head on, was authorised in 1866.

Building began in 1871, but much of it proved unsatisfactory. Work was suspended in 1873 when money ran out, and also over problems with the contractor.

The NER leased the line from July 1, 1875, and hired new contractors to finish the job. The main contractor was John Waddell, but because so much work needed to be redone, the scheduled opening date of July 13, 1881, was missed. Several bridges were defective

and piers out of vertical. The original tunnels were out of line so that when boring was done from either end they did not meet in the centre.

Furthermore, sections of the proposed route were dangerously close to the cliff edge. The NER drew up alternative plans for a route further inland through Sandsend and Kettleness tunnels.

The line finally opened on December 3, 1883, being run from the outset by the NER, which fully absorbed it in 1899.

SOUTH TO SCARBOROUGH
The Scarborough & Whitby Railway was one of several schemes to link both towns by rail.

The Scarborough and Whitby Railway company's bill was passed in the House of Commons at the third reading in April 1865, but the 19¼-mile line was not built because of lack of money.

New proposals emerged in 1870 while the Whitby to Loftus line was being developed.

The latest scheme involved a line starting at Larpool Hall near Whitby, with a 1-in-40 gradient to a station at Hawsker, with more intermediate stations at Bay Town (Robin Hood's Bay), near Fyling Hall, at Hayburn Wyke, Cloughton and Burniston, then Scoresby, and a terminus near West Parade in Scarborough. Parliamentary powers were obtained on June 29, 1871, and building of the 20½ mile route began on May 4 the following year.

The most dramatic engineering feat of this route was the stupendous 13 arch 915ft brick Larpool viaduct over the River Esk near Whitby.

The line was opened on July 16, 1885, and was operated by the NER until 1898. The NER then bought the railway for £261,633, less than half the sum it cost to build.

Throughout its operational lifetime, the Scarborough and Whitby line became notoriously difficult to work. The junction layouts at both ends of the line (Prospect Hill in Whitby and Falsgrave in Scarborough) meant that trains had to reverse direction in order to gain access to the route.

These movements, particularly in the steam era, proved time-consuming and held up the movement of other trains. This problem was worst at Scarborough, where Central station was extremely busy during the summer months.

Below: A section of the North Eastern Railway's tile map of its system, which was mounted on walls at many of its stations. It shows the final network of the company's lines around Pickering. ROBIN JONES

Above: NER G CLASS 4-4-0 No. 557 passes the short-lived Kirby station between Pickering and Marishes Road. JOHN MINNIS/NYMR ARCHIVES

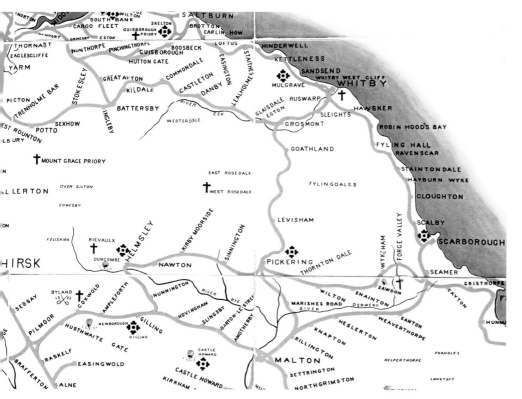

Furthermore, the route line was steeply graded in both directions, up to 1-in-39, and its coastal location meant that the rails were often slippery with rain and sea mists. This made driving conditions in poor weather extremely difficult and great skill was needed from the engine crews to prevent trains from stalling on the climbs.

PICKERING – THE JUNCTION STATION

Originally the southern terminus of Stephenson's line, Pickering ended up as a junction.

In addition to the southern 'extension' to Malton via Rillington Junction, just south of the town lay a double junction at Mill Lane.

Turning east was the Forge Valley line to Scarborough.

The Scarborough & Whitby Railway drew up plans to build a connecting line from Ayton through the Forge Valley, but because landowner Lord Londesborough raised some objections, it was not built. Seizing the opportunity, the NER applied for powers to construct the line between Pickering and Scarborough.

The line served villages between the two towns. Its first train departed from Scarborough at 6.45am on May 1, 1882.

Running west from the Mill Lane double junction was the NER's route which served Kirbymoorside, Helmsley, Gilling, ending at Pilmoor on the East Coast Main Line. An alternative route to York, this very much rural byway of a line opened in 1875.

NEW LIFE FOR BECK HOLE INCLINE

As we saw earlier, the NER built a new deviation line to bypass Stephenson's Goathland incline, so that the entire Whitby to Pickering line would be worked by locomotives throughout.

The incline was abandoned south of Beck

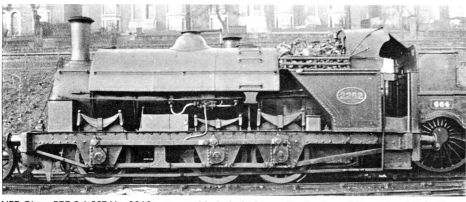

NER Class 577 0-6-0ST No. 2262 was used to help trains up the incline at Goathland. Rebuilt from a Class 93, it was showing its age here (circa 1900). WHITBY MUSEUM/NYMR

Hole, but the northernmost mile and 69 chains was retained as a branch from what became known as Deviation Junction to serve isolated communities.

In June 1872, the Leeds locomotive builder Manning Wardle used the abandoned incline to test one of three 3ft 7½in gauge Fell locomotives which it had built for the 1-in-13 Cantagalo Railway in Brazil, and which used a centre third rail gripping system to help with both adhesion and braking.

The tests were successful, but it was the last time that locomotives ran on the southern stretch of the incline.

While the NER opened the Goathland deviation in 1865, it also built a north to east curve laid at Rillington Junction, allowing trains to run from Whitby via Pickering to Scarborough, but saw such little use that it was closed within a year. The later coastal route between Whitby and Scarborough did the job much better.

THE BLACK COUNTRY OF THE MOORS

When the term North Yorkshire Moors Railway is mentioned today, for many people it conjures up first thoughts of big powerful main line steam locomotives hauling trains through rugged but romantic upland scenery, which has its finest hour when it is clad in purple heather with a blue sky overhead.

Then there are the idyllic little moorland villages which can either be accessed by the railway or on foot from one of the stations. Indeed, if you want a walking or rambling holiday, it is ideal to base yourself at Whitby or Pickering for a week and rely entirely on the heritage railway for transport, using it to access a different location each day for upland treks.

The natural scenic splendour is a major part of the heritage line's tourist appeal.

However, it was not always this way.

When the Whitby & Pickering Railway was promoted, backers talked about its ability to carry fertiliser to uncultivated parts of the moor and create new arable land. Indeed, from the opening of the horse-worked railway in 1836, Grosmont had a set of lime kilns for producing fertiliser, with limestone brought in by rail. Later, George Hudson envisaged the line as bringing trainloads of tourists to his new seaside spa resort on Whitby's West Cliff.

However, the North Eastern Railway saw the Malton to Whitby and connecting lines as creating a rail corridor of heavy industry as mines and quarries sprang up alongside them to tap into the moors' vast mineral resources.

Iron smelting works, brickworks and quarries were linked to the railways by their own branch lines, some of which were substantial narrow gauge concerns. NYMR archivist Mark Sissons, who has extensively researched the largely forgotten industrial landscapes along the line, said that at times there were 40 private sidings or branches between Malton and Whitby, one of the smallest being a very short freight spur which served the village Co-op shop in Grosmont, accessed via a wagon turntable. Even North Riding County Council had a siding at

Grosmont village in the 1870s was dominated by the Bagnall ironworks. FRANK SUTCLIFFE

Above: Goathland station in 1905. On the right is the whinstone crushing plant served by a 3ft gauge tramway.
JOHN MINNIS COLLECTION

Right: The remains of the Pelton wheel for the whinstone crusher at Goathland.
MARK SISSONS

The York & North Midland Railway-built gas works next to Pickering station had its own siding. NYMR ARCHIVES

The old gas works, long since disconnected from the railway, is now a hairdresser's salon.
ROBIN JONES

One of short-lived NER locomotive superintendent Alexander McDonnell's Class 59 0-6-0s hauls a lengthy freight train up the grade into Goathland around 1922.
NIGEL TROTTER COLLECTION.

Fletcher BTP 0-4-4T No. 1342 alongside Whitby signalbox in 1910.
HT BLYAT

Passenger trains return to the Beck Hole branch in 1908.
KEN HOOLE STUDY CENTRE

The North Eastern Railway system at its maximum extent prior to the Grouping of 1923.
ROBIN JONES COLLECTION

MAP OF THE NORTH EASTERN RAILWAY

AT DECEMBER 31st. 1922

North Eastern Railway Company's Lines
including Joint Lines
Running Powers over other Companies' Lines
Other Companies' Lines

Ellerbeck between 1926 and 1960, used for shipping road materials.

It is easy to draw parallels between the North Yorkshire Moors in the 19th and early 20th centuries and Cornwall. Today, the far South West is Britain's top destination for summer holidays in this country, with its sweeping golden sands and surfing beaches, sand dunes, quaint fishing harbours and winding creeks. However, read the small print in the brochures and guidebooks and you will see that Cornwall and West Devon is designated as a World Heritage Site for its mining heritage.

When Cornishman Richard Trevithick invented the steam locomotive more than two centuries ago, the landscape of the Duchy painted a very different picture. It was towering chimneys of tin and copper mine engine houses belching thick black clouds of smoke far and wide, piles of slag heaps, mining families living in conditions no better than squalor and teams of womenfolk, sleeves rolled up, bashing the ore with hammers from dawn to dusk to extract the minerals as an essential part of the process – and not a bucket and spade or wetsuit in sight. Cornwall then would have been much nearer in character to the Black Country or South Wales at the height of its coal mining industry than Hawaii or southern California.

The same was true for the industrial corridor that grew up around the Malton to Pickering railway.

Iron ore had been worked on the moors for centuries, but it was Stephenson's building of the railway that led to the discovery of a vein where the line crossed the Murk Esk just south of the tunnel at Grosmont. By 1875, the village had three blast furnaces, and a slag processing plant later appeared. The NER owned the rights to the ironstone under the river bridge, and ownership of them is now held by the NYMR. There was also a mine and ironstone works at Beck Hole in the middle of the 19th century, and one in Newton Dale.

Sandstone and whinstone were quarried in the Esk Valley, with the Whitby Stone Company exporting it to London. North of Grosmont, a brick and tile works was in use until the 1950s.

Several of the industrial concerns built their own narrow gauge tramways and rope-worked

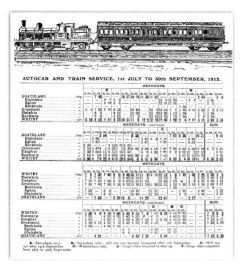

AUTOCAR AND TRAIN SERVICE, 1st JULY TO 30th SEPTEMBER, 1912.

A 1912 timetable for Whitby to Goathland autocar services. NYMR ARCHIVES

A rake of four-wheeled wooden-bodied NER coaches at Whitby in 1900.
KEN HOOLE COLLECTION

inclined planes for taking stone and ore to the nearest transhipment points. One of the most extensive of these systems was to be found at Goathland, where whinstone was quarried.

The 3ft gauge line, which dates from around 1875 and which had a gravity-worked incline, with horses otherwise hauling the wagons, worked into the 1940s.

North of Pickering were three sidings which served local limestone quarries and processing plants. In 1919, a 2ft gauge line was built by the Pickering Sand Company to carry sandstone 2½ miles from a pair of quarries at Saintoft, the exchange sidings at Newbridge, which also had a brickworks. Using steam, petrol and diesel locomotives at various times in its existence, this line was used until October 1961. The presence of such 'tributary' lines invited comparisons with Snowdonia and its world-famous narrow gauge lines, although nobody has as yet seriously suggested reviving one of those serving the Whitby to Pickering route as a heritage line!

THE BOOM TIMES

By Edwardian times, the rail network radiating from Whitby was in place, and for the lines serving the port, there were many years of prosperity. Improvements in conditions for the working class and a new prosperous middle class with more money to spend finally saw George Hudson's tourist dreams for Whitby bear fruit big time. The seaside was a big draw, not only for holidays but also for day trips by train from the northern industrial cities. Despite the proliferation of industrial installations, the influx of visitors also found the moors attractive.

The summer trade led to shuttle services being introduced on the Beck Hole branch, run by steam trains in push-pull fashion, with a locomotive at one end capable of being controlled from a cab in a coach at the rear. In 1908, a small wooden platform was built to accommodate these services, which ran up to the outbreak of the First World War on September 21, 1914.

Such trains, referred to as 'autocars', which allowed a train to be run without the need for a run-round loop or turntable, as is the case with the much later diesel multiple units, also ran between Whitby and Goathland. ∎

An autocar, with the Fletcher BTP 0-4-4T sandwiched between two specially adapted carriages, pictured at the little Beck Hole platform in 1908. KEN HOOLE STUDY CENTRE

Right: Off to war: the local Territorial Army unit waits to depart from Pickering station for the Western Front in 1914. S SMITH/ BECK ISLE MUSEUM

Below: Whitby station frontage in 1920. FRANK SUTCLIFFE/ WHITBY LIBRARY

CHAPTER 4

THE BIG FOUR YEARS

During the First World War, Britain's railways were placed under the direct control of the Government as an emergency measure to ensure that the nation's valuable resources were best directed to the places where they were needed the most – and that did not include competition between routes serving the same destinations.

State control remained until 1921, by which time there were calls to take the more than 100 railway companies that made up Britain's network into permanent national ownership. That would happen 27 years later, with the creation of British Railways, but in the early Twenties it was widely considered a step too far, despite the proven benefits of pooling resources to improve efficiency and cut costs.

Instead a blueprint was drawn up by Eric Campbell Geddes, who had worked with the Baltimore & Ohio Railroad before returning to England and joining the NER. There, he rose to the position of deputy general manager by 1911, and by 1920 was Minister of Transport.

He too saw the prewar competition between smaller railway companies as wasteful, but was opposed to outright nationalisation on the grounds that a monopoly would result in poor management. Instead, he was in favour of creating privately owned regional monopolies through amalgamations,

in other words, grouping the smaller railways into larger companies.

The Railways Act of 1921, which received Royal Assent on August 19 that year, called for the creation of four major companies, the LMS,

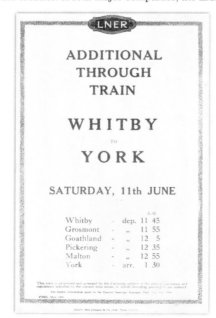

A LNER handbill for an additional York to Whitby through train in 1927. NYMR ARCHIVES

the LNER, the GWR and the Southern Railway, into which most of the country's railway companies would be absorbed or merged.

The Whitby & Pickering route, which was owned by the NER, duly became part of the LNER. The principal other constituents of the LNER were the Great Eastern, Great Northern, Great Central, Great North of Scotland, Hull & Barnsley and North British railways. In total it had 6590 route miles, of which the NER contributed 1757.

The second largest of the 'Big Four' companies, and which would become world famous for its chief mechanical engineer Sir Nigel Gresley's world record-breaking locomotives such as A1/A3 Pacific No. 4472 *Flying Scotsman* and A4 Pacifics No. 2509 *Silver Link* and 4468 *Mallard*, the LNER never made a profit, partly because it inherited huge debts incurred by the Great Central Railway in building its extension to London. Indeed, the LNER had the lowest net revenue per route mile of all the Big Four companies.

THE LNER CUTS ITS CLOTH

When the LNER came into existence on January 1, 1923, for Whitby, Pickering and Malton travellers, it appeared a seamless takeover, but cracks were soon beginning to show.

Left: The A8s were rebuilt from NER chief mechanical engineer Sir Vincent Raven's H1 4-4-4Ts by Nigel Gresley between 1931-36. During the mid-1920s, A8 4-6-2Ts were ordered for the LNER's North East Area to work alongside the H1s. The A8s showed that they had superior adhesion because of their six-coupled driving wheels. In 1931, H1 No. 2162 was rebuilt as a 4-6-2T and reclassified A8. After a series of trials all of the remaining H1s were rebuilt as A8s. They were used on heavy suburban traffic and long-distance coastal trains, replacing the elderly G5 0-4-4Ts. Outshopped from Darlington Works on February 28, 1934, No. 1531 was withdrawn as BR No. 69852 on December 31, 1959. CA DAVIES/MAURICE BURNS COLLECTION

Firstly, the double-track Whitby & Pickering line had been singled between Pickering (Newbridge) and Levisham on New Year's Eve 1916 to provide track materials for use on the Western Front.

According to various stories, some of the track materials were sunk in the English Channel, and other quantities were said never to have left the country, leading to the Government refusing to pay the full amount of compensation. Accordingly, after much deliberation, the LNER decided in 1926 to leave this stretch of the line singled... and so it remained.

Also, there were early closures in the locality, notably the Malton to Gilling line in 1930, and Rillington station itself along with other intermediate stations on the York to Scarborough line the same year.

While passenger and freight usage of the Whitby to Malton line had peaked in Edwardian times, there was a steady fall-off in ticket sales during the LNER period, and freight suffered badly during the depression of the Thirties. Demand for the iron ore and stone quarried from sites along the route dropped, and road transport was making serious progress.

At the end of the First World War, vast amounts of Army surplus lorries and trucks came on to the market at cheap prices, allowing returning servicemen to set up their own haulage businesses in competition with the railways, undercutting them and offering greater versatility.

LNER Gresley D49/2 4-4-0 No. 235 *The Bedale* with a Whitby-York passenger service passes a J23 0-6-0 on freight duties at Levisham on November 6, 1935. No. 235 was built in June 1932 and was withdrawn in August 1960 from Hull Dairycoates as British Railways No. 62740. NYMR ARCHIVES

Sentinel steam railcar No. 22 in varnished teak livery pauses at Whitby during trials on April 6, 1927. It was later named *Brilliant* and painted green and cream. HGW HOUSEHOLD/NYMR ARCHIVES

A Sentinel steam railcar stops at Goathland in the 1930s. NERA

Nonetheless, seasonal patronage of the line boomed. The LNER encouraged regular summer holiday specials from the conurbations of West Riding to Whitby and along the coastal routes to the port with cheap excursion fares. The line from Malton to Whitby became a major holiday route, but sadly, outside the season, ticket sales fell sharply.

The LNER also introduced camping coaches, the first appearing in 1933 when redundant Great Northern Railway wooden-bodied six-wheelers were converted. Four were allocated to the Whitby to Malton route. Eventually, such camping coaches were based at many stations on the network around Whitby including Levisham and Goathland.

The LNER had, like the other Big Four companies, inherited an assortment of stock from constituent companies, and inevitably it was soon time to replace locomotives and coaches. One example of a type which had passed the sell-by date were the BTP (Bogie

Tank Passenger) 0-4-4-Ts which had been built during the tenure of Edward Fletcher as NER locomotive superintendent between 1854-83. These had been used to with one or two coaches to provide 'minimalist' passenger services in the Whitby area since 1905. The LNER looked to replace this set-up with new steam railcars.

STEAM RAILCARS MAKE THEIR DEBUT

The Great Western Railway did not invent the steam railcar, but from early Edwardian times built up the biggest fleet in the country, and is most popularly associated with the concept, which it called SRMs (Steam Rail Motors).

The sole-surviving operating example in Britain today is No. 93, wonderfully restored and rebuilt by the Great Western Society at Didcot Railway Centre in Oxfordshire.

The ancestor of diesel railcars and multiple units, they were a bridge between steam locomotion and internal combustion-powered traction.

They were introduced to counteract competition from trams and buses that could stop anywhere, and therefore serve more passengers.

The basic concept was a steam motor bogie built into a carriage, which could be controlled from either end. In essence they were an all-in-one vehicle that did not need a run-round loop or turntable, unlike conventional steam trains. Furthermore, they could use much shorter platforms, often built as basic halts of one or two coach lengths.

At first, they were a dazzling success for the GWR, which saw passenger numbers soar on lines where they were introduced. However, they became victims of their own success: as extra seats were demanded, they were not powerful enough to haul more than one trailer coach or at best two, and the steam engine compartment was difficult to access for maintenance purposes.

Eventually, the GWR looked to using a detachable coach with a driving cab in the rear for many of its branch line services, and most

LNER G5 0-4-4T No. 381 heads a Malton to Whitby service past Water Ark in 1935. Built at Darlington Works in 1901, the locomotive became No. 67330 at nationalisation and was withdrawn from Malton shed on New Year's Eve 1952. M BRAITHWAITE/WHITBY MUSEUM

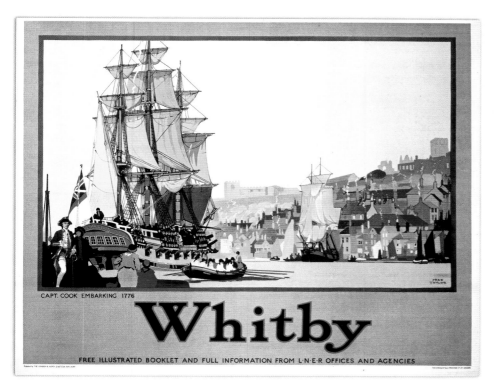

CAPT. COOK EMBARKING 1776

Whitby

FREE ILLUSTRATED BOOKLET AND FULL INFORMATION FROM L·N·E·R OFFICES AND AGENCIES

LNER A6 4-6-2T No. 686 and G5 0-4-4T No.1739 (rear) at Whitby locomotive shed on June 3, 1935. Wilson Worsdell designed the W class tanks after finding that the G5s, the NER's standard passenger tank locomotive, were not powerful enough for the Whitby to Scarborough line. Between 1907-08, he built 10 of them especially for this line.
These were the first six-coupled passenger tank locomotives used on the NER. On the coastal line, they proved themselves to be highly capable at a time when summer passenger traffic was growing, but did not carry sufficient coal and water. Between 1914-17, all 10 were accordingly rebuilt with larger bunkers and water tanks, necessitating the fitting of a trailing wheel making them into Pacific tanks. They became Class A6 under LNER ownership.
H C CASSERLEY

other companies that had bought railcars began withdrawing them by the 1920s.

However, the concept enjoyed a significant revival in LNER territory. Shrewsbury-based manufacturer Sentinel produced a new design with high-speed engines. Sentinel built its first steam railcar in 1923 for the 3ft 6in gauge Jersey Railways & Tramways Ltd, with Cammell Laird of Nottingham supplying the carriage body.

Sentinel exhibited a second railcar at the British Empire Exhibition in 1924, and it attracted the attention of LNER chief mechanical engineer Nigel Gresley.

The LNER was searching for vehicles that would be cheaper to operate than conventional steam trains but which could carry more passengers than the Raven petrol-electric autocars and similar vehicles under consideration.

Between August 17 and 31, 1924, the LNER borrowed a railcar from Sentinel for trials in the North East. The experiment, which involved trials over the steeply graded Whitby to Pickering line proved successful and led to the LNER honouring a prior agreement to

A railcar powered by a NER BTP 0-4-4T at Goathland on August 3, 1925. KEN HOOLE STUDY CENTRE

WHITBY

IT'S QUICKER BY RAIL

ILLUSTRATED GUIDE FREE FROM DEPᵀ· A THE SPA, WHITBY OR ANY L·N·E·R AGENCY

A freight train pulls into Levisham station in 1930. NYMR ARCHIVES

G5 0-4-4T No. 1886 at Levisham in 1937. Built in 1900, this locomotive was shedded at Malton at nationalisation in 1948, and was withdrawn eight years later. NYMR ARCHIVES

order two lightweight railcars with larger boilers in December that year. The first car, No. 41, was delivered in July 1927 on an experimental basis, running between Lincoln and Woodhall Junction, and took the name *Pilot* when it was renumbered two years later as 2121. Its first proper allocation saw it operate on the York-Whitby-Scarborough-York circuit.

Eventually, the LNER bought 80 Sentinel railcars between 1925 and 1932.

Most of the Sentinel railcars had a single engine equipped with a vertical water tube boiler. The cylindrical boiler had an outer shell with an inner firebox, with coal fed through a chute at the top, on to the grate at the bottom of the firebox.

One big advantage over earlier railcar types was that the firebox was designed to be comparatively easily removed without having to lift the boiler out.

All of the Sentinel steam railcars were named after old stagecoaches. Most of them carried a notice detailing information about the stagecoach and offering a reward for further information, recalling the days of Dick Turpin!

The Sentinel railcars suffered from boiler maintenance problems, especially with the water-feed arrangements, and the collection of sediment due to inaccessibility of the washout holes near the base of the boiler.

The drive chains were found to stretch over time, and frame movement owing to a lack of stability inherent in the design led to engine alignments being out of sync. Rising maintenance costs and Second World War

austerity measures resulted in the withdrawals of all the LNER sentinel railcars by 1947.

As with many other rural railways that had been in decline for many years, the Second World War brought about a resurgence in traffic to serve the needs of the war effort, with the Big Four placed under state control.

Whitby was bombed by the Luftwaffe on the night of September 16, 1940, and sizeable damage was caused to the approach to the station. The goods warehouse was also badly hit, and offices near the engine shed were destroyed, while a crater was left in the middle of running lines.

LUFTWAFFE ATTACKS GROSMONT AND PICKERING

However, an all-out effort saw the line running again within a few hours.

A bomb left a hole in the roof of Grosmont station house, although nobody was killed.

An early-morning train from York was targeted by a Luftwaffe fighter as it neared Pickering, leaving one passenger dead. The same aircraft then turned its attention to the Pickering coal yard.

The railways were starved of cash during the war, despite having to carry more traffic. The divergence of resources elsewhere led to many routes being left in dire need of maintenance, and the LNER was all but broke.

The scene was set for cutbacks on rural lines such as those which served the North Yorkshire moors, and the spectre of closures would hang over the hills like a black cloud for the next two decades until the worst happened. ∎

LEVISHAM

Levisham village, as depicted in the LNER's sixpenny guide, *Rambles on the Yorkshire Coast and Moors* by John Hornby, who wrote: "Think of yourself roaming over leagues of heather, picnicking in a bee-loud glade, scampering over bright clean sands, bathing in a sunlit sea. Think of the folk, hospitable and homely; the varied industries of sea and shore, of vale and hill; and lastly, the blithe and bracing air that brings new zest to existence and makes of life a joy. Yes! I think you'd better try the coast of Yorkshire and its heather-scented moors. Then you'll understand the inner glow and unspoken splendour of my theme."
ROBIN JONES COLLECTION

CHAPTER 5

NATIONALISATION
British Railways and Beeching

Following its postwar election landslide, Labour's Attlee government kept its promise to take the nation's railways into public ownership. Accordingly, on January 1, 1948, the LNER became part of British Railways, and the Whitby to Pickering route now became part of the North Eastern Region.

Once the new administration settled in, the pruning of twigs and minor branches began.

The first cutback was the withdrawal of services between Pickering and Scarborough along the Forge Valley route in 1950. By 1948, summer services had been reduced to just three trains a day and many expected the inevitable, which happened on June 3, 1950. A sub-section of the route stayed open for stone traffic from Thornton Dale Quarry until January 25, 1963.

Then came the anachronism that was the Beck Hole branch from Grosmont, which since the First World War had suffered from sharply declining levels of freight, compounded by the

non-replacement of one of the 1847 bridges over the Murk Esk which had been washed away in the floods of 1931. It lingered on, bringing groceries and bare essentials to the remote and isolated hamlet of Esk Valley. In September 1951, the little branch was replaced by a public road built by North Riding County Council.

Pickering was left with another branch service, the cross country route to York via Gilling and Helmsley. Down to just two trains each way per day, the passenger services were withdrawn on January 31, 1953, although the section between Gilling and Kirbymoorside stayed open for freight and specials until August 7, 1964.

The problem faced by Britain's rural railways was a gradual shift from rail to road, which set in after the First World War when vast quantities of army surplus vehicles came on to the second-hand market, allowing entrepreneurs to set up one-man haulage

businesses in competition with winding branch lines. A lorry was often cheaper to run and more versatile and, unlike trains, could make deliveries from the source to the customer.

Unlike the United States which had begun the shift from steam to diesel traction in the Thirties, postwar austerity Britain decided that it could not afford such a move. So British Railways chief engineer Robert Riddles set about building new classes of steam locomotive as a stopgap measure until the time was right. Between 1951-60, a total of 999 of his 12 Standard types were built.

However, as the financial straitjacket loosened, Britain looked to the future, taking on board the fact that railways had to be made far more attractive to customers if they were to compete with road alternatives.

On December 1, 1954, the British Railways Modernisation Plan was unveiled, with the aim of increasing speed, reliability, safety and line capacity, while completely phasing out steam

Whitby shed in the early Fifties. In the foreground is William Worsdell J25 0-6-0 No. 65663, built at Gateshead and entering traffic on December 31, 1898. In 1948 it was shedded at Hull Dairycoates. It was withdrawn from Heaton shed on April 30 and scrapped at Darlington Works. NYMR ARCHIVES

A British Railways poster promoting Whitby as a holiday destination. NRM

haulage in favour of diesel and electric alternatives.

The report also proposed the closure of more unprofitable lines and routes which duplicated others.

One such line which 'doubled up' was the Stockton to Whitby route via Picton and the Esk Valley. The route between Stockton and Battersby saw its passenger services withdrawn on June 14, 1954, with an increase in services from Middlesbrough to Whitby via Battersby Junction, which performed much the same role for longer-distance passengers. The Picton to Stokesley section was closed completely.

In 1956, a government White Paper confidently stated that modernisation would help eliminate BR's financial deficit by 1962. However, the Modernisation Plan failed because it merely tried to upgrade the existing railway so that it would leap ahead of road transport rather than looking at the changing needs of customers in a changing world. And despite its implementation in the second half of the Fifties, with large numbers of first-generation diesels replacing steam across the country, British Railways' losses continued to mount.

In 1954, Britain was one of only seven out of 17 major European countries whose railways were not 'in the red'. The following year, it recorded its first working loss. The

annual working deficit in 1956 was reported as £16.5 million, but by 1962 it had reached £100 million.

Many historians have blamed the mass switch from rail to road not necessarily on the Modernisation Plan but on the ASLEF (Associated Society of Locomotive Engineers and Firemen) national rail strike of 1955.

As the period of austerity receded and the British economy boomed, unions became stronger, and backed by the threat of strike action, they were able to demand better wages and working conditions... and get them.

Just days after Anthony Eden's Conservative party won its General Election victory in 1955, ASLEF called a strike over its demands for a pay rise which amounted to around the price of an extra packet of cigarettes per week.

The strike lasted from May 28 to June 14, bringing Britain and its industry all but grinding to a halt. Members of the public were forced en masse by necessity to find other means of transport, liked what they found and never returned to pre-strike methods. Few predicted the severity of the outcome of the strike, but the damage proved irreparable.

The strike signalled a mass transition by both passengers and freight customers from rail to road.

In previous decades, when rail had a monopoly on passenger transport and the

Thompson B1 4-6-0 No. 61071 leaves Whitby with an evening train to Leeds on July 22, 1958. Built by the North British Locomotive Company in Glasgow and outshopped on August 29, 1946, it was based at Hull Botanic Gardens shed in 1948 and was withdrawn from York North on February 11, 1963, being scrapped at BR's Darlington Works soon afterwards. NYMR ARCHIVES

BR Standard 3MT 2-6-0 No. 77012 passes Darnholm with an 8.55am Whitby to Malton Service in 1957. Outshopped from Swindon works on June 30, 1954, it was withdrawn from York North shed on June 30, 1967, and cut up at the Garnham, Harris & Elton scrapyard in Chesterfield. None of the 20 examples of this mixed traffic design survive, although the 77021 Locomotive Group has been formed to build a new one. NYMR ARCHIVES

The junction for the branch to Newbridge Quarry in the early 1960s. NYMR ARCHIVES

Bog Hall signalbox at Whitby in the Fifties. NYMR ARCHIVES

delivery of freight, the union may have had its way, but now with car ownership on the increase and more rural bus services and freight carriers, its pistol against the public and the Government's head was by now firing only blanks.

Pick-up goods services, which provided a vital supply line to North Yorkshire villages, were hit hard in the reaction to the strike.

The inability of the Modernisation Plan to claw back the promised £85 million a year, coupled with a desire to prevent the country ever being held to ransom by rail unions again, saw national transport policy finally shift from rail to road.

Next to fall victim to the pre-Beeching axe was the winding and scenic coastal route from Whitby via Staithes and Sandsend to Loftus. Popular with summer visitors, patronage fell sharply during the winter months, and British Railways claimed that the five viaducts were too expensive to maintain. It closed on May 5, 1958, although the line was retained from Loftus for freight to Boulby to the present day.

Around this time, British Railways played what it thought would be a trump card, and which did produce some positive results on several lines – the replacement of steam trains with Diesel Multiple Units. Sleeker, swifter and costing less than the corresponding steam train

to run, they were seen as a means of luring passengers back on to rail.

The move did lessen losses on lines where they were introduced, but did not totally eradicate them.

Their introduction in many rural routes was soon seen as a valiant but vain bid to swim against the tide.

With the coastal route north of Whitby West End station closed, DMUs were introduced on the line from Scarborough to the town, running on to Goathland and also to Middlesbrough via Battersby.

Whitby West End station, into which DMU services reversed, was closed from June 12, 1961.

That year, a name little known in railway circles rose to prominence.

The October 1959 General Election saw the appointment of Ernest Marples as Minister of Transport. He favoured road building as the way forward to serve Britain's transport needs, and indeed his family had vested interests in motorway construction.

An independent advisory panel chaired by industrialist Sir Ivan Stedeford was appointed to examine the structure and finances of the British Transport Commission.

Among its members was a Dr Richard Beeching, a physicist and engineer at Imperial

Chemical Industries (ICI) who had been recommended by Sir Frank Smith, ICI's former chief engineer.

Following the panel's recommendations, Marples presented a White Paper to Parliament in December 1960, calling for the splitting of the British Transport Commission into a number of bodies, with the railways being run by a new British Railways Board. It also set financial targets for the railways, which would lead to cuts.

Despite brief encouraging figures around the turn of the decade, in 1961 the railways' annual losses had reached nearly £87 million.

On March 15, 1961, Marples told the House of Commons that Dr Beeching would become the first chairman of the new British Railways Board, from June 1 that year. His remit: stem the losses by making drastic cuts in the system if necessary.

During the week ending April 23, 1962, a key study commissioned by Beeching was carried out by his staff. The findings showed that 30% of route miles carried just 1% of passengers and freight, and half of all stations contributed just 2% of income. Furthermore, half the total route mileage carried about 4% of the total passenger miles.

From the least-used half of the stations, the gross revenue from all traffic did not even

A8 4-6-2T No. 69889 passes beneath the road bridge at Sleights with a Whitby to Middlesbrough service on May 24, 1955. P COOKSON

cover the cost of running the stations themselves.

The writing was clearly on the wall for many rural railways.

The study provided the basis for Dr Beeching's report, The Reshaping of British Railways, which was published on March 27.

Railwaymen had seen traffic dwindle to a trickle or nothing on many routes and already the withdrawal of services could not be avoided, but the sheer scale of the proposed closures sent shock waves throughout Britain.

In short, the 148 page report called for a third of the rail network to be closed, with around 5000 route miles of 18,000 ripped up. Also many other lines were to lose their passenger services and remain open for freight only.

The fundamental argument of the report was that railways should be allowed to do what they did best, and stop competing with road transport in areas where the latter could perform better.

If the full implications of the Beeching report had been implemented, the clock would have been turned back to the days before George Stephenson, and left Whitby without any rail connection as far as passengers were concerned. The three routes, from Malton via Rillington Junction and Pickering, from

Middlesbrough via Battersby Junction and from Scarborough, would be closed to passenger trains, although the Esk Valley line would be retained for coal traffic. A section of the Scarborough line from Whitby including the track over Larpool Viaduct would be retained for potential traffic from a potash mine at Hawsker Bottoms.

The demise of the rural railway in itself was not Beeching's fault. Indeed, thousands of miles of lossmaking routes had been steadily closed by the British Railways region over the previous decade: his report streamlined and accelerated the process by providing a standard national criteria for line closures.

The closure proposals for all three routes were published in February 1964. British Railways produced figures which showed that the line which made the biggest loss was Malton to Whitby, which recorded an annual deficit of $49,200. For every $1 taken in income, $2.45 had to be spent to run the line. It was followed by the Scarborough line, which lost $30,700, and the Esk Valley route, which was $23,000 in the red.

Local people had the chance to appeal against proposed closures to a regional Transport Users' Consultative Committee, which held public hearings at which grievances could be aired and evidence of potential

hardship presented. A record 2260 objections to the closures were lodged in Whitby, including one from the former Whitby Urban District Council.

The Yorkshire Area Transport Users' Consultative Committee hearings took place in Whitby on July 8-9, 1964, with one of the outspoken opponents being Conservative MP Sir Alex Spearman, defying his Government.

Arguments presented in favour of retaining the Whitby to Pickering route included bad winter weather on the moors which restricted road transport and the need for children in Goathland to use the train to get to school. Traders in Whitby also feared a negative impact on tourism.

The TUCC found that closing both the line from Malton to Whitby and the Esk Valley route would cause great hardship.

Local people widely expected the main route from Whitby to York via Pickering to be saved. However, on September 11, 1964, just a month before the General Election, and maybe with one eye on voters, Marples confirmed the closure of both the routes to Malton via Pickering – but reprieved the line to Middlesbrough via the Esk Valley.

It was certainly an unusual choice. While the wonderfully scenic Esk Valley route serves several isolated villages, it was far from being

Before Harold Wilson became Prime Minister, his Labour Party candidates vowed to reverse the Beeching cuts if they came to power. Labour won the 1964 General Election and not only kept Beeching on, but eventually closed more lines than he had recommended the year before.

Below: LNER K4 2-6-0 No. 3442 *The Great Marquess* arrives at Whitby with a filming special on March 3, 1964. NYMR ARCHIVES

the most direct link between Whitby and the main population of Yorkshire. Marples said that he made his decision based on the importance of Whitby retaining a rail service to link it to the nearest large centre of population, in this case Middlesbrough, the importance of the tourist trade to the port and the surrounding area, and the extreme difficulty of operating buses over the Esk Valley roads to serve the villages and schoolchildren, especially in winter. It was far from ideal for bringing in holidaymakers, but a winding railway was, as far as Whitby was concerned, better than no railway at all.

As part of his election campaign, the Labour candidate for Scarborough and Whitby produced a pledge signed by none other than Harold Wilson himself that the remaining closures to Whitby would not go ahead if his party won the election.

Somewhat surprisingly in retrospect, the Beeching closures barely featured in the election campaign.

Within a month, Wilson was in Downing Street, ending more than 13 years of Conservative control, but had only a majority of four seats, and it was clear that Wilson would soon need to go to the polls again to obtain a comfortable working majority.

Looked upon to redeem Labour's pre-election pledge with regard to Whitby, new Transport Minister Tom Fraser claimed in the House of Commons on November 4 that due to a technicality in the 1962 Transport Act, he was powerless to reverse his predecessor Marples' decisions – despite the fact that they had not yet been implemented.

Neither did Wilson appear inclined to intervene with a state-controlled industry. His election 'pledge' was not worth the paper on which it was written.

Yes, Britain's railways were losing money hand over fist, and looking at the trends in other countries where rural branches were subject to mass closures, it seemed that cutbacks would be made regardless of who was in power.

Yet the question arises time and time again – why does the electorate still heed election promises?

However, there was no widespread uproar over the apparent U-turn. Indeed, many sections of the press were in support of Beeching's attempts to reduce the burden on the taxpayer by ridding the country of sizeable parts of a transport system which was by natural forces of supply and demand becoming obsolete

The Fraser regime carried on where the Marples one had left off, and Beeching, still on a five-year secondment from ICI, retained his post. Indeed, in the coming years, the Labour Government made rail closures over and above those listed in the Beeching report.

Fraser stated that he had asked British Railways to retain the track on closed lines where there was no immediate need for them to be ripped up or sold off. British Railways was also asked to retain Goathland to Grosmont in case schoolchildren were marooned by snow. Indeed, the line was regularly inspected by a signalling trolley.

The breathing space afforded by Fraser allowed the redundant line to survive long

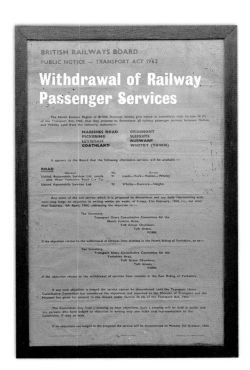

The closure notice for the Whitby to Malton route posted in 1962. NYMR ARCHIVES

Dr Richard Beeching's report, The Reshaping of Britain's Railways, published on March 27, 1963, broadly called for the closure of a third of the national network's route miles, including all routes to Whitby. NRM

J25 0-6-0 No. 65690 at Bog Hall on June 19, 1951. Built by the NER at Gatehead on January 1900, it was based at Hull Dairycoates shed at Nationalisation in 1948, and was withdrawn from Whitby shed on November 11, 1954. No member of the class survived into preservation. A G FORD

B1 4-6-0 No. 61276 stands on Whitby's Bog Hall turntable on May 14, 1964. JOHN BOYES/J W ARMSTRONG TRUST

Built for the NER in 1900, William Worsdell G5 0-4-4T No. 67308, seen at Pickering shed in the early Fifties, was a veteran of the Whitby to Malton line. At Nationalisation it was shedded at Whitby, and it was withdrawn from Malton shed on New Year's Eve 1955. It was scrapped at Darlington Works shortly afterwards. NYMR ARCHIVES

enough until would-be revivalists emerged.

In the meantime, anti-closure protests continued, with local Liberal candidate Richard Rowntree – who later became a chairman of the North Yorkshire Moors Railway – organising a protest train.

However, the date for closure was set by British Railways as March 8, 1965. All that was needed was for the replacement bus services to be approved by the Road Traffic Commissioners, which was done in February.

The last day of operation was set as March 6 that year, and was marked by a heavy snowfall,

with blizzard conditions at the summit of the Malton-Whitby route enar Moorgates.

Preserved LNER K4 2-6-0 No. 61994 *The Great Marquess* and K1 2-6-0 No. 62005 hauled the 'Whitby Moors' special organised by the Stephenson and Manchester locomotive societies. It ran over the routes from Whitby firstly to Scarborough and then to Malton via Pickering.

The last train of all running south from Whitby to Malton was the 6.54pm service which was hauled by Class 40 D259 – a surprise choice as a DMU had been expected –

Rebuilt from a Raven H class 0-4-4T at Darlington Works and re-released into traffic on February 29, 1936, LNER 4-6-2T A8 No. 69852 stands at Pickering, minus its original trainshed roof, in the Fifties. The locomotive was shedded at Whitby shed (50G) at the dawn of the British Railways era, and withdrawn on November 30, 1959, being scrapped at Darlington within a month. As no A8s made it into preservation, what a marvellous subject for a future new-build project the type would make, especially if it ran on the North Yorkshire Moors Railway! NRM

LNER A8 4-6-2T No. 69861 approaching Pickering with a Malton to Whitby train on April 4, 1957. The A8s became redundant following the introduction of diesel multiple units, and were all withdrawn between 1957-60, when the class became extinct. As an A8, No. 69861 dated from August 31, 1935, when it emerged from Darlington Works, and was withdrawn from Malton shed on June 30, 1960. It was scrapped at Darlington. IAN ALLAN LIBRARY/CG PEARSON

A DMU passes Bog Hall signalbox as it pulls into Whitby with a Middlesbrough-Scarborough service. MAURICE BURNS

B1 4-6-0 No. 61275 arrives at Whitby station, then named Whitby Town, with the 4.08pm service from Malton on May 18, 1964. JOHN BOYES/JW ARMSTRONG TRUST

Farewell special: heading the 'Whitby Moors' special organised by the Stephenson and Manchester locomotive societies. K4 2-6-0 No. 3442 *The Great Marquess* and No. 62005 Whitby pass beneath Larpool viaduct in fading light on the double-track line to Levisham. MAURICE BURNS

LNER A8 No. 69861 at Goathland with a Malton to Whittby Town train in 1958. NYMR ARCHIVES

while the final northbound train, the 5.55pm from York to Whitby, comprised a Metro-Cammell DMU.

The line north of Rillington Junction was retained to serve New Bridge Quarry and the coal yard at Pickering.

It was also used on June 3, 1965, when the Royal Train, headed by LNER V2 2-6-2 No. 60886, was stabled overnight at Marishes Road station when the Duke of Edinburgh visited the nearby Fylingdales Early Warning Station. A large crowd gathered when the empty stock ran into Pickering for the V2 to run round – it had probably been the largest

steam engine to use the line prior to the heritage era.

The line was woken with a jolt following a heavy snowfall on November 29, 1965, which as predicted left Goathland schoolchildren stranded with their bus unable to take them home. British Railways ran an emergency DMU service. The passenger train from Whitby to Goathland on the afternoon of November 30, 1965, was the last that British Railways ever ran over the line.

The final freight working south of Pickering to Malton ran on July 1, 1966, headed by class 03 shunter D2066. ■

Class 40 D259 hauling steam-heated non-corridor coaching stock arrives at Grosmont with the 8.55am Whitby-Malton train on March 5, 1965. MAURICE BURNS

By-then-preserved K4 No. 3442 *The Great Marquess* and K1 No. 62005, then still owned by BR and shedded at York, wait in the sidings at Whitby prior to working the 'Whitby Moors' special to York and Leeds on March 6, 1965. MAURICE BURNS

The last-ever BR passengers to use Pickering station catch the final train, the 6.54pm Whitby to Malton, on March 6, 1965, without an enthusiast in sight! Yet it would not be the end… MAURICE BURNS

The end… or was it? On the evening of March 6, 1965, *The Great Marquess* and No. 62005 depart Pickering for York and Leeds. Gaslit Pickering station would see just two more trains before total closure, the northbound 5.55pm York to Whitby Town and the southbound 6.54pm Whitby Town to Malton. MAURICE BURNS

The first section of former British Railways track in the north of England to be reopened was the Keighley & Worth Valley Railway. The National Collection's LMS 'Crab' 2-6-0 No. 42700 is seen arriving at Oxenhope on November 3, 1968, its first year of operation. JOHN WHITELEY

PRESERVATION:
Going it alone

No. 2 *Dolgoch* was the only operational steam locomotive available to the Talyllyn Railway revivalists in 1951, and was therefore the engine that started the operational heritage railway movement. ROBIN JONES

The end of steam and the modern era of Britain's railways saw a wheel turn full circle. From the relaunch of the Talyllyn Railway by volunteers in 1951, there have been numerous examples of people wanting to save a particular route from closure, in the belief that it could be made to pay with services restored.

Many such initiatives led to Britain's portfolio of more than 100 heritage lines, all run by their own companies. In this respect, it has been a return to the formative years of the national network, when individual lines big and small began as independent concerns, before amalgamations and mergers took place, ultimately leading to the Big Four at the Grouping of 1923 and British Railways in 1948.

Today's volunteer-led preservation section is a magnificent monument to 'people power', the desire by people to prove to the powers that be that they were wrong in closing a particular line, and the affection that it had accrued over the generations by those who had come to rely on it.

The North Yorkshire Moors Railway may be the most popular of all our steam lines, but it was by no means the first, or even among the first generation of those to be saved.

LBSCR 'Terrier' 0-6-0T No. 55 *Stepney* departs from Sheffield Park with the Bluebell Railway's first public service on August 7, 1960. BLUEBELL RAILWAY ARCHIVES

The blueprint was set by the saving of the Talyllyn, prompted by by the author and biographer Tom Rolt, who in 1950 wrote a letter to the *Birmingham Post* suggesting that the little 2ft 3in gauge line in mid-Wales could be saved by ordinary people. Sufficient interest was mustered for a meeting to be held in the Imperial Hotel in Birmingham on October 11, 1950. A committee was formed which within a fortnight was talking to the executors of the estate of Haydn Jones, who had owned the line before his death.

The Talyllyn Railway Preservation Society took control of the line on February 8, 1951, and by May had attracted 650 members. The line reopened under the society's wing on May 14, 1951, and in doing so, planted an acorn which grew into the mighty and massive oak tree that is the heritage railway movement today.

WHERE IT REALLY BEGAN
However, Rolt and the Birmingham-based Talyllyn saviours did not invent railway preservation.

That may be deemed to have begun back in 1839, when Robert Stephenson & Company's Canterbury & Whitstable Railway pioneer locomotive *Invicta*, the next to be built after *Rocket*, and the first to work on a public railway south of the Thames, was set aside for posterity after just six years' service.

Rocket itself was preserved in 1862, albeit in a much-changed form.

The 50th anniversary of the opening of the Stockton & Darlington Railway was marked by the North Eastern Railway with an exhibition at Darlington in 1875 and six years later, the centenary of George Stephenson's birth was marked with the assembly of a static display of veteran locomotives at Newcastle, including *Invicta*.

From such beginnings, several locomotives were preserved either by museums or railway companies themselves. The 1925 Stockton &

Darlington Railway which included a cavalcade of 53 locomotives and trains, old and new, was followed by an exhibition at Faverdale Wagon Works, from which the older engines were taken to York, to form the nucleus of the country's first dedicated railway museum, set up by the LNER.

A major milestone was marked in 1927, when the Stephenson Locomotive Society preserved LBSCR 0-4-2 No. 214 *Gladstone* – it was the first time a locomotive had been saved by enthusiasts.

However, while saving locomotives and stock in itself is commendable, it is still a long way from taking a closure-threatened branch line into independent ownership, either by volunteers or a commercial concern.

INDEPENDENT RAILWAYS: THE LAST WAVE
The Light Railways Act of 1896 may be viewed as the milestone which would in a very different and later era provide the platform for volunteer enthusiast-run lines to spring up across the country.

The principal aim of the act was to facilitate the provision of cut-price railways with a maximum speed of 25mph, just like today's preserved lines, to serve the populations of rural areas where potential profits were so minimal that established railway companies were not interested in serving them.

A plethora of short lines sprang up across Britain in the wake of the act, and with one or

The Severn Valley Railway's first public services ran on May 23, 1970, with GWR Collett 0-6-0 No. 3205 hauling the inaugural train from Bridgnorth to Hampton Loade. SVR ARCHIVES

The first Dart Valley Railway public services crosses Nursery Pool Bridge on April 5, 1969, with GWR pannier tank No. 6412 sandwiched between two sets of auto coaches. Following an early Nineties buyout by its supporters' association, the line is now the South Devon Railway. SW LINES

two exceptions, marked the last significant wave of 'railway mania' in this country, until the modern-day building of High Speed 1, the Channel Tunnel Rail Link.

Many of these light railways had striking similarities with today's heritage lines, using second-hand engines and stock, often rendered obsolete by the march of progress elsewhere and would otherwise have been consigned to Victorian or Edwardian scrapyards.

The key figure in the light railway boom was Colonel Holman Frederick Stephens, who as an engineer built several lines including the Rye & Camber Tramway, the Selsey Tramway, the Rother Valley Railway, taking over others, including the Weston, Clevedon & Portishead, Ashover Light, Edge Hill Light, Kent & East Sussex, Shropshire and Montgomeryshire Railway, Snailbeach & District Light and Festiniog (then spelled with one 'f') and Welsh Highland railways, amassing a sizeable empire before his death on October 23, 1931.

Stephens, however, did not advocate lines being run by enthusiast volunteers, and kept

them just about ticking over before the post-First World War growth in road haulage forced many such concerns to close.

The latter concept originated with the concept of the miniature railway, with replica main line locomotives built to a fraction of the size of the prototype initially for the amusement of the rich.

ENTER THE ENTHUSIAST

Landowner Sir Arthur Heywood had a 15in gauge line running on his estate in 1874, with the idea of selling it to a wider audience. In 1895 he built such a system at Eaton Hall for the Duke of Westminster.

This particular line drew the attention of one Wenman Joseph Bassett-Lowke, who was to become the most famous modelmaker of the early 20th century.

Bassett-Lowke was already familiar with a passenger-carrying miniature line at Blakesley Hall near Towcester which linked the mansion to the local railway station, using two imported US-outline 4-4-0 steam locomotives. With the

aid of engineer Henry Greenly, Bassett-Lowke formed a company, Miniature Railways of Great Britain, in 1904.

Many rich enthusiasts longed to own and drive their own steam locomotives, but any main line railway would have been utterly horrified by such a request.

Bassett-Lowke's business enabled such dreams to be fulfilled, and established the principle of a small railway line that was owned, managed and driven by one or more enthusiasts.

In 1915, Bassett-Lowke turned his attention to the derelict 3ft gauge Ravenglass & Eskdale Railway in the Lake District, which he saw advertised for sale in the *Model Engineer* following its closure to passengers in 1908 and freight in 1913. He bought the line, which ran for seven miles from Ravenglass up into the Cumberland hills, and which had been England's first public narrow gauge railway when it opened in 1875. He re-laid it to 15in gauge.

An assortment of locomotives and stock was brought in to run on it, and so came about the Ravenglass & Eskdale Railway that we know today.

Bassett-Lowke repeated the procedure at the 2ft gauge horse-drawn tramway, which carried passengers from the Barmouth ferry on the south side of the Mawddach estuary in Wales, to the tiny seaside village of Fairbourne. The tramway opened in the early 1890s to serve a local brickworks, while horse trams serving the emerging seaside holiday trade were introduced in late 1898. Bassett-Lowke also converted this line to 15in gauge, reopening it in 1916 as the steam-operated Fairbourne Railway complete with his locomotives.

Bassett-Lowke had exceeded the limitations of a miniature railway for either a private estate or a seafront or park line for popular amusement, to produce fully-fledged public passenger-carrying railways in their own right and both had been developed on the trackbed of previous lines used for a purpose other than tourism, and both had been revived with the enthusiast in mind.

It was First World War pilot Captain John Edwards Presgrave Howey who pursued a project to recreate a main line in miniature. His Romney, Hythe & Dymchurch Railway opened in 1927 and soon had a total length of 13½ miles, making it for decades the world's smallest public railway and the longest 15in gauge operation.

The Romney Hythe & Dymchurch Railway's 1925-built Davey Paxman 4-6-2 No. 1 *Green Goddess* on the last lap on its journey to Hythe on August 29. The RHDR was the ultimate in miniature railways where the owners could drive their own steam locomotives and run their lines independently of any large company. ROBIN JONES

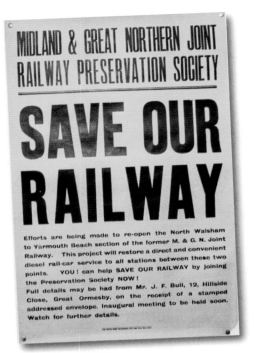

SOUTHWOLD RAILWAY TRAIN.
SEP 1879 - APRIL 1929.

A postcard of a train headed by Southwold Railway Sharp Stewart 2-4-2T No. 1 *Southwold*. In 1929, the line so nearly became Britain's first preserved railway. ROBIN JONES COLLECTION

An early Midland & Great Northern Joint Railway Society poster asking for support for its initial bid to save the North Walsham to Yarmouth Beach section of the system. It later switched its attention to the line west of Sheringham to Melton Constable, which closed in 1964.

FULL-SIZE TAKEOVERS

So when you next visit a heritage railway, you can see that the principles on which it was founded share some DNA with the seaside miniature lines that were commonplace throughout much of the 20th century.

Yet the building of such lines for amusement as a prime motive cannot, at least in its day, be considered heritage, but more a microcosm of the full-size prototype.

Historic miniature railways have attracted the 'heritage' tag only with the passage of time, and by default.

None of them were examples of preserving existing railways exactly as they were, and none relied on volunteer labour. That key stage was still decades away.

Twenty-two years before the Talyllyn volunteers ran their own trains, a bid was made to save the 3ft gauge Southwold Railway in Suffolk, which closed in April 1929. Local resident and railway engineer Ron Shepherd drew up a blueprint to save the 8½ mile line and presented it to the Ministry of Transport and the local council the following month.

The plan involved him buying part of the line and raising the rest of the cash through a bonds issue. He amassed a consortium including local councillors and some wealthy locals.

Once the railway was acquired, steps would be taken to buy Sentinel steam railcars to provide the efficient and attractive passenger service that the line had lacked for so long that it had become a popular music hall joke.

Yet the owning company refused to negotiate a deal with Shepherd or anyone else, and appeared determined to see it remain closed. The locomotives and stock remained where they stood until 1942, when they were scrapped for the war effort and the line lifted.

However, in the years that followed, several of the aforementioned established historic concepts came together. In the August 1934 issue of *The Railway Magazine*, reader E Hill suggested reopening the recently closed Welsh Highland Railway, regauging it and running it with miniature locomotives like the Ravenglass & Eskdale. He wrote: "Any railway enthusiast with means could probably buy the whole concern and with energy and suitable advertising, build up a successful service."

The January 1941 issue of *The Modern Tramway*, the journal of the Light Railway Transport League, contained a letter from Manchester reader Arthur E Rimmer, asking if the Welsh Highland passenger service could be reintroduced to save petrol supplies. If its reinstatement on commercial grounds was found to be not possible, would it be practicable for clubs and societies supplying free labour to tackle such a scheme, he asked.

The late poet laureate, Sir John Betjeman (right), visited Tywyn Wharf station on the pioneer Talyllyn Railway in 1965, and is seen in the company of founder Tom Rolt.
TR ARCHIVES

"That established a principle of fundamental importance," said Owen Prosser, one of the founders of the Talyllyn Railway Preservation Society. "As far as I know, it had never been suggested before."

The scene was therefore set for the Talyllyn milestone of 1951.

AFTER TYWYN

Many may have considered the Talyllyn revivalists as eccentrics or weekend hobbyists, but the impact of their actions proved resounding… eventually.

At first, the response of the public to the idea of taking over a closure-threatened railway may have appeared slow. Indeed, it hardly seemed relevant, for in 1950, there was no immediate threat to steam traction on the national network or the prospect of wholesale closures of large swathes of it. Nobody in railways had heard of Dr Richard Beeching or the British Railways'

The Whitby & Pickering Railway had been running for only three years at the time, but railway preservation may be deemed to have begun in 1839 when Robert Stephenson's 0-4-0 *Invicta*, built for the Canterbury & Whitstable Railway, was withdrawn and offered for sale. When no buyer was found, it was placed in storage and eventually became an exhibit in Canterbury Museum. ROBIN JONES

Modernisation Plan and the first of 999 BR Standard locomotives was yet to appear. So why would anyone want to save an obscure slate-carrying line in the hills behind Tywyn?

However, the saving of the Talyllyn provided a gem of inspiration to Ealing comedy film producers. The 1953 classic The Titfield Thunderbolt starring Stanley Holloway and Sid James, in which villagers take over a branch line faced by closure using an antique locomotive, proved a massive box office hit and dragged the rail revival concept into the public consciousness.

On July 23, 1955, the first heritage-era trains ran on the part of the otherwise derelict Festiniog Railway, which businessman Alan Pegler had bought the year before with the aim of reopening it as a tourist line. Alan would later make history in 1963 by buying LNER A3 Pacific No. 4472 *Flying Scotsman* from British Railways.

Following the failure of public campaigners to save the Lewes to East Grinstead Railway, on March 14, 1959, a group met in Ardingly and formed a society which soon changed its name to the Bluebell Railway Preservation Society.

It failed to buy the whole line, but settled for a section between Sheffield Park and Horsted Keynes to run not as full-blown public services but as an animal of a different kind, a tourist attraction, with vintage locomotives and stock operated by unpaid volunteer staff. In 1960 the section from Sheffield Park to Bluebell Halt, 100 yards south of Horsted Keynes, was opened. It was the first section of the national network to be reopened by volunteers.

However, the Bluebell volunteers were pipped at the post by students from Leeds University under the direction of their professor, Fred Youell, who in June that year began running public services on the nearby Middleton Railway which therefore became the first standard gauge railway of all to be taken over and operated by unpaid volunteers.

The idea of rail revival was now planted in the mind of the general public, and in the years of the Beeching closures of the early Sixties, and the imminent eradication of steam haulage, it would come to the fore again and again.

When the Keighley to Oxenhope line was closed in 1961, local people formed a preservation society to buy it, reopening it in 1968 as a heritage railway.

In South Devon, a group of businessmen who saw that soon there would be a public demand for a line on which people could once again ride behind steam locomotives began looking into the possibilities of taking over a branch line when it closed. Moretonhampstead and Kingsbridge were considered, but in the end the Totnes to Ashburton line came up for grabs, and became the Dart Valley Railway, running its first services in 1969, when it lost the section north of Buckfastleigh after the building of the new A38 trunk road.

Dart Valley Railway plc subsequently bought the Paignton to Kingswear line straight out of British Rail service, taking it over from January 1, 1973.

Looking at the Bluebell example, enthusiasts in the West Midlands looked for a line in the Kidderminster region to save, and

Tom Rolt, the man credited with starting the volunteer-led heritage railway movement, alongside Talyllyn Railway No. 2 *Dolgoch*, being driven by David Curwen at Tywyn Wharf station on May 14, 1951, when the Talyllyn Railway Preservation Society ran its first trains to Rhydyronen. TR ARCHIVES

The Keighley & Worth Valley Railway opening special of June 29, 1968, was hauled by Ivatt 2-6-2T No. 41241 and SR USA 0-6-0T No. 72. GAVIN MORRISON

chose the Severn Valley Line running south from Bridgnorth which closed to through passenger and freight services in 1963. Heritage services began in 1970 from Bridgnorth to Hampton Loade, extending to Bewdley in 1974 and Kidderminster in 1984.

In 1959, when pre-Beeching British Railways announced that the entire 160 mile Midland & Great Northern Railway system would close, it sent shock waves through the national network. It was the first time in history that a complete system was to close.

The Midland & Great Northern Joint Railway Society was formed with the intention

of saving all of it. Such aspirations were rapidly edited, and in 1965, it began work on restoring arguably the most picturesque section of the system, what is today's North Norfolk Railway, running from Sheringham to Holt.

Against the background of the successful preservation schemes, none of which can be said to have restored year-round passenger services as run by British Railways, but instead set up heritage lines as attractions rather than local transport amenities, a bid to save Grosmont to Pickering began in the aftermath of its closure by Dr Beeching. ∎

CHAPTER 7

TO THE SUMMIT AND DOWN AGAIN!

The revival of Grosmont to Pickering 1967-73

The controversy caused by the demise of the Whitby to Pickering line did not die down: indeed, the cudgel was taken up by local newspaper the *Whitby Gazette*.

Eventually, Labour Transport Minister Barbara Castle despatched a junior minister to look at the Goathland situation in early 1966, but again her prime minister's pre-1964 general election pledge was forgotten and the line remained closed.

Although British Rail, as it had been rebranded by then, had been told it could not lift the track immediately, it was revealed that by 1967 it was preparing to do so that summer in the absence of any local council grant aid to reopen either the Malton or Scarborough lines.

Yet local people were not prepared to lie down and take it without a further fight.

Tom Salmon, who had wondered how to fight the closure plans as soon as Dr Beeching announced them, set up a meeting at his home in Ruswarp on June 3, 1967, to see if anything could be done at this late stage to save the line to Pickering.

Several local railwaymen who were familiar with the line attended the meeting. Among them was retired BR driver Fred Stuart, a county councillor from Whitby who had fought the closure and who had even suggested using the rates to subsidise it.

In true The Titfield Thunderbolt fashion, he said: "If BR or the local authorities will not operate it, can we try?"

The similarity with the Ealing comedy lay in the fact that the group's aims had more to do

The Newcastle University Railway Society's 1898-built E Borrows of St Helens well tank No. 3 approaches Green End en route for Goathland with a Hull & Barnsley Railway coach prior to a 'blow-up' at Darnholm on April 27, 1969. Clearly too small for use on today's NYMR, this little engine, which worked at Wallsend slipway, is now in storage at the Tanfield Railway pending overhaul. JOHN BOYES/J W ARMSTRONG TRUST

with community use of the line than following in the footsteps of the Talyllyn or Bluebell railways and reopening it on a preservation basis. The group's target was Grosmont to Pickering and members told British Rail about their aims.

This action had the desired effect of stopping the lifting of the track south of Grosmont, as the

transport minister had first to be informed of any such expressions of interest. At a packed public meeting at Goathland on November 18, 1967, the North Yorkshire Moors Railway Preservation Society was established, with Fred as its first chairman and Tom as secretary. Already there were 450 members, such was the support for the reopening of the route.

NER P3 0-6-0 No. 2392 showing four red lamps and Lambton 0-6-2T No. 29 take the Royal Train into Grosmont, where the Duchess of Kent boarded on May 1, 1973. JOHN BOYES/J W ARMSTRONG TRUST

The signalman looks out of the original Grosmont signalbox to see the arrival of the NYMR's first motive power – AC Cars diesel railbus No. 79978 – on August 9, 1968. JOHN BOYES/J W ARMSTRONG TRUST

The founders of the North Yorkshire Moors Railway, including Tom Robertson, Harold Blackburn, John Randall, Tom Salmon, Fred Stuart and Michael Pitts. TOM SALMON COLLECTION

Volunteers laying track at Levisham in 1972. MAURICE BURNS

Mirvale shunts a load of machine tools at Grosmont on April 12, 1970. Many of Britain's top heritage railways started out with industrial shunters: the first services on the Middleton Railway at Leeds in 1960, for example, were hauled by a diesel. *Mirvale* is now based on the Middleton Railway. C DAVIES

Salmon heads a works train seen unloading a sheerleg on May 21, 1970. C DAVIES

The North Eastern Locomotive Preservation Group handed over newly restored NER P3 0-6-0 No. 2392 to the NYMR at Grosmont station in October 1971. The station at the time retained its junction signalbox and the locals still hung their washing line over the tracks! JOHN BOYES/J W ARMSTRONG TRUST

BREATHING SPACE

While the wonderfully scenic coastal route from Whitby to Scarborough was by then being dismantled, British Rail agreed to hold off on the Malton route for six months while the society became established.

British Rail asked for £120,000 for the route from Grosmont to Pickering, including the track. The sum was way out of reach of the embryonic society, which was given six months until April 1, 1968, to come up with a viable scheme.

British Rail then agreed to sell the land between Grosmont and Pickering, along with a single line of track as far south as Ellerbeck, for £42,500. The remainder of the track would be lifted.

The society set its stall on reopening the 5½ mile Grosmont to Ellerbeck section, with a new halt being provided near Fylingdales to provide access to the National Park, as well as a terminus and run-round loop at Ellerbeck. Tourists were now seen as the initial major source of custom.

The first item of rolling stock arrived on August 9, 1968, in the form of AC Cars diesel railbus No. W79978. In the late 1950s, British Railways tested a series of small railbuses, produced by a variety of manufacturers, in a bid to cut the costs of running rural branch line trains. While many proved to be very economical, some were also unreliable.

The lines they worked on were mainly closed by Beeching and, being nonstandard, they were all withdrawn in the mid-1960s.

Salmon and Borrows No. 3 take on water at Ellerbeck during their northbound move on March 30, 1969. A bucket chain had to be formed to refill their tanks. JOHN BOYES/JW ARMSTRONG TRUST

British Rail bought five from AC Cars, and W79978, which was built in 1958, served on the Scottish and Western regions until it was withdrawn in 1968, making the journey from Grangemouth to Grosmont over the national network under its own power. It may seem astonishing today that the world's most popular steam heritage railway began

with diesel traction. It was followed by a first class sleeping car to be used as volunteer accommodation.

From November 10 that year, British Rail allowed working parties to access the line using maintenance trolleys. Around the same time, a new company, the North Yorkshire Moors Railway Ltd, was formed.

The North Riding County Council special train on July 23, 1971, stands at Pickering where driver Chris Cubitt shakes hands with Alderman J Fletcher, chairman of NRCC, while Lord Downe (left) and Richard Rowntree (right) look on. This meeting effectively led to the saving of the track from the summit to Pickering. MAURICE BURNS

AC Cars railbus No. 79978 passing the remains of Newtondale signalbox with a Goathland to Pickering (High Mill) train on a members-only gala weekend in 1970. JOHN BOYES/J W ARMSTRONG TRUST

FIRST STEAM

On January 25, 1969, the NYMR's first steam locomotive arrived at Pickering. It was privately owned 1955-built Hudswell Clarke 0-4-0ST named *Mirvale*. It steamed from Pickering to Grosmont, with British Rail's permission, attracting big crowds in the process.

Following shortly afterwards were Barclay 0-6-0ST Salmon and Borrows 0-4-0WT No. 3 of 1898, owned by the Newcastle University Railway Society, on March 28.

Early the following year, the British Railways Board approved the sale of the whole line complete with track to the summit at Ellerbeck and the trackbed only to Pickering.

May 19, 1969, saw another big milestone, with a 10% deposit of $4250 paid on the purchase of the line.

In the second half of 1969, British Rail singled the double track section of the line between Grosmont and Levisham. The move sparked a race against time to buy the

The North Eastern Locomotive Preservation Group's NER Q6 0-8-0 running as LNER No. 3395 hauls a Grosmont to Goathland summit members-only train past Darnholm, comprising Hull & Barnsley and LNER Thompson stock in August 1971. MAURICE BURNS

Volunteers laying the main crossover at Grosmont minus bright orange high-visibility vests which were not a statutory requirement in 1970. JOHN BOYES/J W ARMSTRONG TRUST

AC Cars railbus W79978 is cleaned by 17-year-old volunteer Nick Carter at unrestored Goathland station prior to the all-important trip by North Riding County Council to Pickering on October 26, 1969. JOHN BOYES/J W ARMSTRONG TRUST

remaining single track line through Newtondale, the glaciated gorge seen as a major tourist draw for the railway.

At this stage the North Riding County Council and the North York Moors National Park Authority enter the scene. The planning committee persuaded British Rail to hold off lifting the remaining track to Pickering. On October 21, 1969, No. W79978 was allowed to run all the way from Grosmont to Pickering with Fred Stuart, a county councillor and former Whitby locoman, driving. On board was the county planning officer. After the trip he agreed to ask the park authority to support the county council in persuading British Rail to hold off lifting the track. The park authority for its part did not want a terminus in the middle of the moors and felt it was better that the revived line should go all the way to Pickering.

The NYMR was encouraged to aim straight for Pickering and in return the county council suggested that it could buy the track from British Rail.

In late 1969, the second track on the line was lifted by British Rail, with Class 40 D399 heading the scrap train back to Malton on November 2.

Following further talks, British Rail applied for a Light Railway Order under which the NYMR could run trains. While waiting for the powers to run public trains, the revivalists manoeuvred round the problem by offering travel through the purchase of membership tickets on the day. *Mirvale* and *Salmon* became the stars of an Easter 1970 steam gala which British Rail allowed to be held at Goathland, and not only did it raise vital funds for the NYMR, but also led to a series of frequent steaming weekends.

Many heritage railways, including some of today's biggest, started out by running industrial locomotive types, wholly unauthentic to a main line setting but which satisfied the general public's craving to see steam in the years following its demise on the main line on August 11, 1968.

Mirvale at Ellerbeck en route from Pickering to Goathland on February 2, 1969, the day it arrived on the North Yorkshire Moors Railway. The locomotive worked for Mirvale Chemicals in Mirfield, West Yorkshire. JOHN BOYES/J W ARMSTRONG TRUST

However, more appropriate locomotives for a former North Eastern Railway route were on the horizon.

The North Eastern Locomotive Preservation Group had been busy elsewhere preserving NER P3 (J27) 0-6-0 No. 2392 and T2 (Q6) 0-8-0 No. 63395, and the NYMR was seen as the perfect home. Also arriving in June 1970 was Lambton, Hetton & Joicey Collieries Kitson built 0-6-2T No. 29, followed two months later by Stephenson 0-6-2T No 5 from the same stable.

A steam gala was held on June 27-29 that year, and the Q6 and No. 29 hauled three-coach trains from Grosmont to Goathland, using volunteer BR steam drivers.

On March 27, 1971, the NYMR Preservation Society transformed itself into the North Yorkshire Moors Historical Railway Trust.

John Megson (North Yorkshire Moors Railway treasurer), Tom Salmon (secretary) and county councillor Fred Stuart (chairman) at the May 1969 signing of the cheque for the 10% deposit on the agreed contract with British Railways to purchase the line from Grosmont to the summit and the remaining trackbed to Pickering.
TOM SALMON COLLECTION

The June 1970 steam gala sees *Mirvale* shunting at Goathland. MAURICE BURNS

THE LINE BOUGHT

In early 1971, the British Railway Board agreed a price of £42,500 for the whole 18 miles of trackbed from Grosmont to High Mill, Pickering. The English Tourist Board offered a £30,000 grant towards the line purchase.

By now, membership had risen to around the 6000 mark, and a multitude of fundraising events were staged, from raffles and sponsored walks to collecting Green Shield stamps.

On July 23, 1971, a special train hauled by No. 29's sister engine from the Lambton, Hetton & Joicey Colliery Railway No. 5 ran from Grosmont to Pickering carrying Alderman J Fletcher, chairman of North Riding of Yorkshire County Council, and his guests.

On November 3 that year, the council voted to negotiate with British Rail to buy the 12 mile line between Ellerbeck and Pickering.

The idea was that the county council would buy the track and sell it to the NYMR over 20 years, saving the revivalists from having to relay the line in the future. On New Year's Eve 1971, the North York Moors Historical Railway Trust was formed as a successor to the preservation society and was registered as a charity the following February. In doing so, the NYMR became Britain's first railway to achieve charitable status.

Grosmont was chosen by members as the site for the line's motive power depot and engineering base.

BUILDING BEGINS

Building work began in 1971 and two years later the engine shed came into use. A carriage and wagon works was established to the north of Pickering station, with a shed provided in 1984 to allow work to be done under cover and protected from the elements.

In late 1972, Richard Rowntree, the second heritage trust chairman, informed railway members in the house magazine *Moorsline* that the following year would be very special indeed, for the railway would reopen to the public at large. Several paid staff had been appointed, but more volunteers were needed.

Early 1973 saw a public timetable issued, the intention being to operate steam shuttles between Grosmont and Goathland and a three car Metro-Cammell DMU hired from British rail for trips over the full length of the saved line.

A fresh obstacle arose when Pickering Urban District Council tried to buy the town station and turn it into a car park. While a public inquiry was awaited, a temporary platform was built at High Mill level crossing as a makeshift southern passenger terminus.

The trust then applied to transfer the Light Railway Order from British Rail.

BACK ON TRACK AT LAST!

On Saturday, April 21, charter trains ran over the line. The first timetabled heritage services were run on Easter Sunday, April 22, 1973, with the first public steam hauled train

Borrows No. 3 and *Salmon* crossing the long-vanished crossing at Pickering station on March 28, 1969. JOHN BOYES/J W ARMSTRONG TRUST

Chris Cubbit hand coaling Lambton, Hetton & Joicey Colliery 0-6-2T No. 5 at Grosmont on June 11, 1971. C DAVIES

hauled by No. 2392. The official opening took place on May 1. The Duchess of Kent arrived at Whitby by air to perform the ceremony.

She unveiled a plaque at the Angel Hotel where plans for the Stephensons' original line were made in the 1830s, and after a celebratory lunch travelled by car to Grosmont to be greeted by a large crowd.

It had been hoped to run a special train all the way from Whitby to Grosmont, but it was prevented from doing so by industrial action involving British Rail.

There she unveiled another commemorative plaque and was presented with a painting.

The duchess, whose family home lay in the Howardian Hills, a few miles from Pickering, activated a signal to give the 'all clear' for the seven-coach royal reopening special train, double headed by No. 29 driven by Norman Ash and No. 2392 with Chris Cubitt on the regulator, to proceed.

Worked as a Royal Train, there were 300

The hired-in DMU at the temporary High Mill platform at Pickering on the first day of services. DAVID IDLE/NYMR ARCHIVES Inset: A 30p ticket for the NYMR's first steam train on April 22, 1973. NICK CARTER

LNER Q6 0-8-0 No. 63395 heads a train to the line's summit on June 27, 1970. C DAVIES

invited guests on board. At Pickering, a brass band led the duchess as she walked from the station to the Black Swan Hotel where she unveiled a third plaque.

SUCCESS FROM THE START

By the end of the first season, 73,037 tickets had been sold, bringing in total receipts of £23,636. In 1974, there was a 50% increase in receipts, and more good news came later that year when the public inquiry inspector came down in favour of the railway regarding the plans to flatten Pickering station. It came into NYMR use on May 24, 1975.

In 1976, the trackbed between Moorgates and Pickering was bought by the county council and leased back to the NYMR for a nominal rent. The future was not only looking rosy, but also secure.

In 1975, steam locomotives worked regularly as far south as Levisham, and timetabled steam services all the way to

A snowbound Goathland welcomes Hudswell Clarke 0-4-0ST No. 1882 of 1955 *Mirvale* after its historic move from Pickering on February 2, 1969. JOHN BOYES/J W ARMSTRONG TRUST

Pickering began in 1976, although diesels still played a big part.

In 1981, Newton Dale Halt was opened for walkers to access the moors. Pickering's Up platform was extended in 1990 to cater for longer trains brought about by demand for services, and a third platform face at Grosmont completed in 2004 also boosted capacity.

The line has had to be resignalled, with colour light signals installed around Pickering and eventually a new signalbox commissioned at Grosmont.

From humble beginnings, and the desire of locals not to take their Beeching cut lying down, mighty main line steam locomotives now carry up to 350,000 passengers a year through the magnificent scenery of the national park.

The humble AC Cars railbus No. W79978 left long before the NYMR reached such dizzy heights, and is now to be found at the Colne Valley Railway in Essex. ■

Norman Ash, driver of Lambton, Hetton & Joicey Colliery Railway 0-6-2T No. 29, talks to the Duchess of Kent on May 1, 1973. J BOYES/J W ARMSTRONG TRUST

Above: With the three giant 'golf balls' of RAF Fylingdale's early warning radar base atop Snod Hill on the horizon, railbus W79978 winds its way through the lonely moors. The radar station was built by the Radio Corporation of America in 1962 and consisted of three 40-metre-diameter geodesic domes known as radomes as containing mechanically steered radar. Its primary purpose is to give the UK and US governments warning of an impending ballistic missile attack, part of the 'four minute warning' during the Cold War. A secondary role is the detection and tracking of orbiting objects. Far from being a state secret, the radar station became a landmark and local tourist attraction. When coach tours to Whitby drove past the site, their drivers would switch the radio on and allow passengers to listen to the interference caused by the radars. Between 1989 and 1992, Raytheon, US defence contractor, replaced the golf ball domes with the pyramid structure housing the Active Electronically Scanned Arrays radar. C DAVIES

The 40th anniversary special heads past Green End hauled by Lambton tank No. 29 and K1 No. 62005 on May 1, 2013. MICHAEL ANDERSON

PIONEERS RECOGNISED

It has been often said with infinite justification that without Tom Salmon, there probably would not have been a North Yorkshire Moors Railway.

To mark the 40th anniversary of the opening in 1973, a special train met the surviving three founders of the preservation society who attended its first meeting on June 3, 1967.

Michael Pitts, aged 77, Tom Salmon, 87, and Charlie Hart, 90, were invited to the anniversary train from Whitby to Pickering on May 1, 2013, but on health grounds could not attend

The location had great significance in that the first meeting called by Tom at his home Rosebank where the name North Yorkshire Moors Railway Preservation Society was decided was in Ruswarp and Charlie Hart had been a signalman at the station.

Co-operation and full support from the families, the local pub and Network Rail to man the nearby crossing allowed the special train to stop for five minutes.

The train carrying a 40th anniversary headboard and flags and hauled by NELPG's K1 2-6-0 No. 62005 duly arrived at the station where plaques were presented by the then North Yorkshire

Moors Railway Trust chairman Murray Brown to each of the founders and flowers to Tom's wife Erika.

When Tom Salmon was asked why he first thought the line should be saved, he said the reason was his grandparents living in Thornton-le-Dale would take him, as a young boy, on walks in Newtondale, frequently getting the train home from Levisham.

The beauty of the glacial gorge of Newtondale in the North York Moors National Park through which the railway runs is why he thought the line should be saved.

Appropriately it was Charlie Hart who, using the green flag that was used to give the right of way to the first steam hauled NYMR passenger train in April 1973, symbolically set the 40th anniversary train on its way from Ruswarp to Pickering.

In our picture above, seated are Michael Pitts (left), Charlie Hart (centre) and Tom Salmon, who is being presented with a commemorative plaque by Murray Brown. The back row comprises Tom's daughters Nina and Wendy and granddaughter Natalya and Charlie Hart's son Tony. MAURICE BURNS

Former Ruswarp signalman Charlie Hart gives the right of way to the 40th anniversary special on May 1, 2013, using the same green flag as waved the first official public NYMR train off in 1973.
MAURICE BURNS

Tom and Erika Salmon at Ruswarp station on May 1, 2013. Sadly, Erica died on Christmas Eve that year and was quickly followed by her husband Tom Salmon who died on Christmas morning. General manager Philip Benham said: "The volunteers and staff of the NYMR could not be more grateful for all they both have done for the railway." Locomotives carried wreaths in honour of Tom and Erika during the Christmas and New Year period. NYMR

NER P3 (LNER J27) 0-6-0 No. 2392 (65894) heads past Beck Hole on July 1, 1972. Having arrived on the embryonic heritage line in October 1971, it provided the mainstay of services in the period leading up to the official reopening. PHILIP BENHAM

Sir Nigel Gresley pulls away from Goathland with the 'Wizards Express' on February 18, 2005.
BRIAN SHARPE

STREAKING ACROSS THE MOORS

How many heritage railways can boast one of the most famous operational steam locomotives in the United Kingdom today as a flagship?

The North Yorkshire Moors Railway is the proud home of LNER A4 streamlined Pacific No. 60007 *Sir Nigel Gresley*, the 100th Gresley Pacific to be built, and named in honour of its designer.

A sister to world steam speed record holder No. 4468 *Mallard*, which hit 126mph on Stoke Bank in Lincolnshire on July 3, 1938, No. 60007 holds the postwar record.

Thankfully, six members of the ground-breaking iconic class of 35 have survived into preservation. Plans to save *Mallard* for the National Collection were made in 1960, but sadly, there would be no reprieve from the scrapyard for the first of the class, No. 2509 *Silver Link*, one of the first five 'Streaks' (as they were popularly known) to be withdrawn from British Railways' service, in December 1963.

Three, *Sir Nigel Gresley*, No. 60009 *Union of South Africa* and No. 60019 *Bittern*, were bought by British enthusiasts. Two went to museums in North America. No. 60008 *Dwight D. Eisenhower* to the US National Railroad Museum in Green Bay, Wisconsin, and No. 60010 *Dominion of Canada* to the Exporail museum near Montreal in Canada, saved purely because of their names.

It was the name *Sir Nigel Gresley* which focused a group of enthusiasts on saving No. 60007 after it was withdrawn from main line service in 1966.

The idea of naming the locomotive, LNER No. 4498, after its designer, was the brainwave of K Risdon Prentice, co-author of Locomotives of the LNER 1923-37, published by the Railway Correspondence & Travel Society. If he had not done so, No. 4498 would have, like other members of the class, been given a bird's name, most likely *Bittern*.

After being outshopped from Doncaster Works, with a single chimney and side valances covering its wheels, No. 4498 was first posted to King's Cross shed on November 30, 1937, although the move was not made permanent until February 25, 1938.

From King's Cross, No. 4498 hauled big name trains such as the 'Silver Jubilee', 'Coronation' and 'Flying Scotsman' out of London and earned a name for itself for speed and power.

First appearing in the standard LNER garter blue of the A4 Pacifics with silver gilt letters; new numbers and letters for the tender in stainless steel were added in a general overhaul on January 16, 1939.

The locomotive was repainted into wartime black with LNER markings on February 21, 1942, when the valances were removed as an austerity-era aid to maintenance. The garter-blue livery with red-and-white lining was reapplied on March 6, 1947.

Sir Nigel Gresley was painted into British Railways' dark blue with black-and-white lining and renumbered 60007 on September 27, 1950, following nationalisation, when it was also fitted with Automatic Warning System apparatus. It is this livery that the locomotive was carrying in 2014.

Its last British Railways' colour change saw it repainted into Brunswick green on April 17, 1952.

[Badge: 60007 — POSTWAR SPEED RECORD HOLDER — 112MPH — GAINED 23RD MAY 1959]

The locomotive, reallocated to Grantham between April 1944 and June 1950, featured at the official opening of British Railways' Rugby testing station between August and October 1948. It was placed on to the rollers without its tender and run up to high speeds to monitor the coal and water usage.

DOING A 'MALLARD'?

According to railwaymen's unofficial stories, A4 driver Bill Hoole, who started his career on the Cheshire Lines Committee as an engine cleaner and worked his way up to become a top link driver at King's Cross, was said to have reached 117mph when he took No. 60007 hauling the 'Tees-Tyne Pullman' down Stoke Bank in November 1955.

On board was a civil engineer with a Hallade Track recording instrument, who would have been aware of the 90mph limit having been exceeded, however, the device was not designed for recording such speeds. As such its accuracy was questioned, and so it was not possible to take disciplinary action against the footplate crew over concerns for the safety of the passengers on board.

When built in 1938, *Mallard* was the first A4 to be fitted with a double chimney and double Kylchap blastpipe, an arrangement which improved draughting and exhaust flow at speed (the remainder of the class were retrofitted in the late 1950s, and No. 60007 received its double chimney and double blastpipe on December 13, 1957.

Mallard's record was never broken, as the urge to set new steam records vanished with the Second World War, never to return. By the time the years of postwar austerity

were over, designers were looking ahead to diesel and electric traction, and so the question did not arise again.

This caused some sadness within the enthusiast fraternity, but the march of progress was unavoidable. Nonetheless, to mark its 50th anniversary, the Stephenson Locomotive Society decided to have a celebrity farewell trip for steam on the East Coast Main Line, as it was quickly being taken over by diesels.

Sir Nigel Gresley was selected for the tour, and sent by the Eastern Region to Doncaster Works to be overhauled for the purpose.

Its normal driver Bill Hoole, who on June 3, 1958, had driven *Sir Nigel Gresley* hauling the Royal Train from King's Cross to York with the Queen on board, was duly rostered for the trip.

For the SLS special, British Railways' civil engineers agreed to the speed limits to be

Sir Nigel Gresley, the man, with *Sir Nigel Gresley*, the locomotive. NRM

relaxed over certain sections of the route, with a maximum of 110mph down Stoke Bank, the place where so many historic speed records had been set, including No. 4472 *Flying Scotsman's* run in November 1934, when it became the world's first steam locomotive to officially reach 100mph.

The eight-coach train departed King's Cross on Saturday, May 23, 1959, with fireman Alf Hancox joining Hoole on the footplate.

It was said the locomotive reached 100mph after Stevenage on the outward journey to Doncaster, and ascending Stoke Bank, it hit 83mph between Essendine and Little Bytham.

On the return leg, Stoke summit was passed at 75mph, with the speedometer rising to 99mph before Corby Glen, reaching 109mph by Little Bytham.

Hoole appeared to be going for the record, never mind his alleged earlier near avoidance of disciplinary action. When *Mallard* had achieved the world steam speed record it had been hauling a braking test train, and carrying only railway staff and technicians, who had all been offered a taxi alternative before the record was attempted – and all refused.

When Hoole's train reached 112mph, Alan Pegler, a member of the Eastern Region board who was on the footplate, and who later bought *Flying Scotsman* for preservation, signalled to inspector Bert Dixon that the driver must ease off.

The 12.3 miles from Corby Glen to Tallington were covered in just seven minutes six seconds at an average of 104mph. That in itself was the fastest ever time between those points by a steam locomotive, even faster than *Mallard*.

Beyond Tempsford, 100mph was reached for the third time on the tour. The train arrived back at King's Cross four minutes early having

taken 137 minutes 38 seconds from Doncaster, averaging 68mph over the 156 miles.

Mallard's record-breaking trip had been cut short at Peterborough when the big end ran hot. This time there was no such problem, and *Sir Nigel Gresley* was back in scheduled service within 24 hours.

LAST RECORD CHANCE

From such figures, it seems logical to conjecture that had it been given the chance, *Sir Nigel Gresley* could have beaten *Mallard's* official record on Stoke Bank. As it was, the SLS special was probably the world's last chance to ever see the record broken, although over the years, other non-verified locomen's tales about having unofficially exceeded 130mph with A4s have been aired. Whether or not that is the case, there is no doubt that Grosmont shed today has a very special engine indeed in its care.

After Hoole retired in 1959, he went to work as a driver on the Ffestiniog Railway, which may well be described as today's narrow gauge

equivalent of the North Yorkshire Moors Railway, running through stupendous upland terrain and leading the market in its particular sector. The Ffestiniog had been saved by Pegler in the early Fifties, in the wake of the success of the Talyllyn Railway revival. Hoole died in 1979 and is buried in Minffordd cemetery near the line.

When King's Cross shed closed, No. 60007 was reallocated to New England shed at Peterborough on June 16, 1963.

Shortly afterward, on July 6 that year, No. 60007 hit 103mph when running down Stoke Bank with the Locomotive Club of Great Britain's '*Mallard* Commemorative' railtour.

Another transfer saw it reallocated to St Margarets shed on October 20, 1963. From there, it hauled Edinburgh-Aberdeen trains. Its final allocation was Aberdeen on July 20, 1964, and its last-known duty in revenue-earning British Railways' service was the 5.30pm Aberdeen to Perth run on January 7, 1966.

It was withdrawn on February 1, 1966, having run around 1.5 million miles since new. During its working life for the LNER and BNR, *Sir Nigel Gresley* was fitted with 12 boilers, No. 27966, from No. 60016 *Silver King*, being the last to be fitted, on October 25, 1962, and two tenders, No. 5329 from new and No. 5324 from August 1943.

A group of enthusiasts had earlier vowed to save No. 60007 when the time came, and on October 1964 formed the A4 Preservation Society, taking Pegler's purchase of No. 4472 as their blueprint for how to proceed.

When on October 23, 1965, the society organised a railtour from Manchester to Paddington it asked BR to roster *Sir Nigel Gresley* for the trip.

The group bought the condemned locomotive in March 1966, after which it was sent to Crewe Works for overhaul. At Crewe, it was given the three pairs of 6ft 8in driving wheels from sister A4 No. 60026 *Miles Beevor* because they were in far better condition. Also in the works being cosmetically restored before export to its namesake country was *Dominion of Canada*.

Sir Nigel Gresley leaving Doncaster at the start of its postwar record-setting journey to King's Cross with a Stephenson Locomotive Society special on May 23, 1959. ERIC OLDHAM

A4 No. 4498 *Sir Nigel Gresley* being tested at British Railways' then-new Rugby Locomotive Testing Station in 1948. NRM

Back in LNER garter blue livery, No. 4498 undertook trial runs in early March 1967, and later that month, worked the late-night Crewe to Preston parcels train.

Once the engine was back in traffic, the society turned itself into the A4 Locomotive Society Limited.

That year, *Sir Nigel Gresley* ran a series of railtours. Its first, on April 1, 1967 from Crewe to Carlisle, with later trips to Weymouth and Aberdeen. On July 23 No. 4498 made a comeback to the East Coast Main Line.

When Carnforth's steam shed closed, it became a popular heritage railway museum called Steamtown. From there, once British Rail had relaxed the main line steam ban it had imposed in August 1968, *Sir Nigel Gresley* headed railtours once again.

No. 4498 was reunited with 'speed king' Hoole at Carnforth in April 1972. There, he drove it up and down the half-mile Steamtown running line.

In August 1975, No. 4498 took part in the Rail 150 Cavalcade at Shildon, marking the 150th anniversary of the opening of the Stockton & Darlington Railway, which had inspired Whitby businessmen to press for their own line.

Sir Nigel Gresley was chosen to haul a series of special trains between Marylebone and Stratford-upon-Avon in late January 1985. No. 4498 and *Flying Scotsman* were briefly joined on shed at Marylebone by *Mallard* on October 11, 1986.

In the 1990s the engine became the only A4 to be fitted with steam heating on the front. That allowed it to be run tender first on heritage railways which do not have turning facilities. *Sir Nigel Gresley* remained on the Great Central Railway at Loughborough during the first half of that decade, before moving to the East Lancashire Railway.

In 1995 No. 4498 reverted once again to No.60007 as well as becoming the first steam locomotive of the preservation era to have worked up Shap summit on the West Coast Main Line. Four years later, *Sir Nigel Gresley* hauled a special train to mark the 40th anniversary of its record run down Stoke Bank. Two years later, it was withdrawn for traffic for overhaul.

In 1999, *Sir Nigel Gresley* moved to the North Yorkshire Moors Railway, and soon afterwards its owning group, the *Sir Nigel*

Sir Nigel Gresley lines up alongside unique BR Pacific No. 71000 *Duke of Gloucester* during its visit to the North Yorkshire Moors Railway in April 2011. PHILIP BENHAM

Gresley Locomotive Preservation Trust Ltd, agreed for it to be based there. A new 10-year boiler ticket was obtained following a £810,000 overhaul, partially financed by a Heritage Lottery Fund grant of £332,000. It returned to traffic in the summer of 2006, operated by the A4 Locomotive Society Ltd.

Early in July 2008, No. 60007 joined its three UK-based sisters for a line-up at the National Railway Museum in York, and on June 18, 2012, it carried the Olympic Torch over the NYMR before the opening of the London Games.

Thousands lined the streets of Whitby to watch Scarborough PE teacher, Kelly Williams, carry the flame into the centre of the town. Arriving at the station to cheers and applause, she ran straight on to the platform to the waiting BR standard 4MT 4-6-0 No. 75029 *The Green Knight*. Along with 220 local schoolchildren, she boarded the train for the 20 mile journey to Pickering, as the train departed amid yet more cheers.

At Grosmont, *Sir Nigel Gresley*, carrying a 'NYMR Torch Bearer' headboard, replaced

No. 75029 to take the train to its destination.

The train arrived at 11.34am, and Kelly handed the flame over to University of York student Max Strachan, the first of four torchbearers to carry the flame through Pickering's streets where an estimated 10,000 spectators had gathered.

The following year, No. 60007 was springboarded back on to the international stage when it joined its five surviving sisters for the National Railway Museum's phenomenally successful celebrations to mark the 75th anniversary of *Mallard's* record run.

STREAKS REUNITED

On July 3, 2013 – the exact anniversary – thanks to the efforts of former NRM director Steve Davies and his team, plus a host of other companies involved with the project to temporarily repatriate *Dwight D. Eisenhower* and *Dominion of Canada* from their museum homes in North America in return for cosmetic restoration, all six were reunited around the museum's turntable in the Great Hall, under the banner of the Great Gathering. There were three A4s in LNER garter blue (*Mallard*, *Dominion of Canada* and *Bittern*), two in BR Brunswick green (*Dwight D. Eisenhower* and *Union of South Africa*) and one in early BR lined blue – No 60007. Many visitors said it was the smartest of the six.

It was one of the most spectacular and poignant moments in the history of railway preservation, and attracted visitors from as far afield as New Zealand and a South Pacific island. Nearly three years of planning had finally come to fruition.

The first Great Gathering lasted for two weeks, a second at York from October 26 until November 11 and a third, under the banner of the Great Goodbye, at the Locomotion museum in Shildon from February 15-23, 2014. The net result was 364,400 visitors to the three

Scarborough PE teacher Kelly Williams holds the Olympic Torch next to *Sir Nigel Gresley* at Pickering. NYMR

Sir Nigel Gresley becomes the first steam locomotive to cross the rebuilt Dawlish sea wall with Steam Dreams' 'Cathedrals Express' trip to Kingswear on April 10, 2014. DAVE COLLIER

"IN 1995, NO. 60007 BECAME THE FIRST STEAM LOCOMOTIVE OF THE PRESERVATION ERA TO HAVE WORKED UP SHAP SUMMIT ON THE WEST COAST MAIN LINE."

events and a profit of £650,000 for parent body the Science Museum Group; the two borrowed A4s returning across the Atlantic in May.

In February 2014, the nation was shocked when part of Isambard Kingdom Brunel's South Devon Railway sea wall route at Dawlish was washed away, leaving rails suspended in mid-air and the rail network to the west cut off from the rest of Britain. A marathon effort by a team of 300 Network Rail engineers had the spectacular washout repaired by April 4, and six days later, *Sir Nigel Gresley* added another page to heritage railway history books by becoming the first steam locomotive to cross the rebuilt sea wall.

Heading a Woking-Kingswear 'Cathedrals Express', with steam coming on at Westbury, No. 60007 was greeted as it passed through Dawlish by flag-waving spectators on the bunting-draped platforms and the beach, the A4 sounding its chime whistle in response.

Sir Nigel Gresley returned to Kingswear nine days later, hauling the Railway Touring Company's 'Dartmouth Express'.

So 77 years after it emerged from Doncaster, the locomotive continues to make history, as well as entertaining the crowds of Britain's most popular heritage railway. ∎

North Yorkshire Moors Railway general manager Philip Benham meets Prince Charles at the National Railway Museum in York on July 22, 2013, as part of the Mallard 75 celebrations which involved *Sir Nigel Gresley*. The prince was patron of the event. ROBIN JONES

The six A4s lined up outside the Locomotion museum during the Mallard 75 event on February 21. No. 60007 is on the far left, next to *Dwight D. Eisenhower*. Third from left is *Bittern*, next to *Dominion of Canada*, *Mallard* and *Union of South Africa*. ROBIN JONES

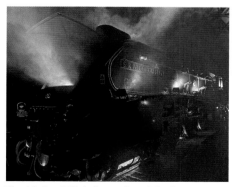

The Mallard 75 Autumn Great Gathering at York encompassed the annual Locos in a Different Light contest. Theatrical lighting students illuminated the six A4s to bring out different aspects of their heritage. Complete with smoke effects, *Sir Nigel Gresley* takes on a surreal deeper-than-usual blue aspect. ROBIN JONES

CHAPTER 9

Stunning scenery
magnificent locon

It was realised by the revivalists from the early days that the scenery of the North Yorkshire Moors Railway would make it a prime destination for visitors.

They could sit back and enjoy the dazzling series of panoramas that look good at any time of the year, and in almost any weather, from the elevated heights of a railway carriage – always the best vantage point from which to enjoy the countryside.

Before the saviours of the route took a deep breath and agreed to go all the way through to Pickering, a shorter line was considered, but landscapes such as Newton Dale with its glaciated gorge were always a 'must' in their minds.

Their vision has certainly been endorsed by the fact that up to 350,000 visitors a year ride on the trains.

However, that is just the tip of the iceberg as far as the local economy is concerned.

As news of the progress being made by the revivalists spread far and wide, more people came to ride on the heritage line.

Yet it has been estimated that many more came to see and photograph the action from the lineside, without ever buying a ticket.

Hard-bitten volunteers might grumble that sightseers enjoying the greatest free show on the moors are simply freeloaders, enjoying the fruits of someone else's labour without paying a penny towards it. On the other hand, every time a lineside cameraman's photograph gets published in the media, be it the mainstream or enthusiast press, it affords invaluable free advertising for the line.

Furthermore, every time someone stops and looks at the line, it means they are more likely to use local services – shops, garages, restaurants and takeaways, and maybe even spend the night in a bed and breakfast establishment or a hotel.

Over the decades, the number of people who have chosen Whitby and the moors, with the railway playing a part in their choice, is incalculable.

The stunning upland scenery leads into the second primary reason for the line's huge popularity.

Steep gradients require powerful locomotives, especially if you want to haul

LEFT: Lambton tank No. 29 crosses Bridge 31 on May 3 during the 2014 spring steam gala. PHILIP BENHAM

Q6 0-8-0 No. 63395 waits to head a freight train into Grosmont as visiting LNER A4 streamlined Pacific No. 60009 *Union of South Africa* leaves Goathland with the 'Moorlander' Pullman dining train on March 30, during the 2008 spring steam gala. BRIAN SHARPE

NER Q6 NO. 63395

The huge upsurge in NER mineral traffic in late Victorian times led to the design of Wilson Worsdell's T1 0-8-0s, but very quickly it became apparent that more locomotive power was required. Sir Vincent Raven designed his T2 class based on the T1 but with a larger boiler, and a total of 120 T2s were built between 1913 and 1921 in six batches. They proved to be a resounding success, giving excellent reliable service until the end of steam.

Initially allocated to sheds in the North East for coal traffic, by 1920 the T2s would occasionally be used for medium- and long-distance freight as well.

The LNER reclassified them as Q6s and they ventured to Manchester via the Woodhead Tunnel, north of the Tyne and south to Peterborough and March.

Withdrawals started in 1963, and the last Q6 was taken out of traffic in 1967.

While NELPG's initial aim was to save a J27, it decided to go for a Q6 too. No. 63395 was among the last in service.

At first, it was housed in the locomotive shed at Tyne Dock when restoration began. It was moved to Hartlepool on September 4, 1968, and on to Thornaby the following February. It first steamed in the heritage era in the roundhouse at Thornaby in October 1969.

No. 63395 arrived on the NYMR on May 26, 1970, and made history as the first main line locomotive, as opposed to industrial types, to be based on the line.

Carrying LNER livery as No. 3395, it featured in the early members' open days hauling shuttle trains from Goathland.

A full overhaul was completed in the summer of 1975 when it reappeared in lined-out NER black as No. 2238.

It was granted a certificate to take part in the Stockton & Darlington 150th anniversary cavalcade at Shildon that August.

The locomotive became a mainstay of NYMR traffic until it was withdrawn for a heavy general overhaul in 1982. It was to remain inside NELPG's Deviation shed at Grosmont for 18 years, with other projects taking priority.

Eventually, the boiler was overhauled with the aid of a Heritage Lottery Fund grant, the job being contracted out to the NYMR. In the meantime, the mechanical overhaul of the frames was carried out at Darlington after being taken by road from the NYMR's permanent way yard at Newbridge, Pickering in January 2002. In October 2006, the boiler passed its official hydraulic test and on November 1 that year was lifted back on to the frame so that the final reassembly of the locomotive could begin.

When it returned to traffic in 2007, the locomotive carried its British Railways identity of No. 63395, following a ballot of NELPG members.

While it is in regular use on NYMR passenger services, its long wheelbase is not ideal for such work on a sharply curving route. However, gradients are no problem: it regularly hauled heavy coal trains up the 1-in-46 Seaton bank from Ryhope up towards South Hetton colliery in County Durham.

The Q6 has also visited a number of other heritage railways.

otives

trains longer than three coaches. Unless you are prepared to use diesel traction – still a minority interest among the general public – large main line steam locomotive types need to be employed.

As we have seen, tank engines such as the G5 and A8 classes which once formed the mainstay of passenger and freight services to and around Whitby are extinct. Accordingly, locomotives far larger than those which would have been seen in regular service on the Malton to Whitby route have by necessity as well as choice been brought in.

The net result: a spectacular combination of big glamorous locomotives running through breathtaking vistas.

Lambton, Hetton & Joicey Colliery 0-6-2T No. 29: an industrial locomotive holding its own among the NYMR's illustrious main line performers. BRIAN SHARPE

THE LAMBTON, HETTON & JOICEY COLLIERY TANKS

Many of today's standard gauge heritage railways had humble beginnings as industrial steam locomotives which never would have run on the main line in British Railways' days, or had simply hauled one or two coaches along a short section of track.

Indeed, when the likes of *Mirvale* and *Salmon* returned steam to the Grosmont to Pickering line in the late Sixties, there was rapturous applause.

The NYMR became a byword for big main line locomotives tackling steep gradients through spectacular moorland scenery, and there was quickly no place for such smaller 'starter' locomotives which could not even try to cope in regular service with the rigorous demands of the line.

However, among the NYMR's collection of main line locomotive types and similarly illustrious visitors, there is a pair of industrial tank locomotives which have become part and parcel of the residential fleet.

The Durham coalfield was criss-crossed by a labyrinthine network of railways in its heyday. Interspersed with it were several private lines leading from the main line to a colliery or works.

In some cases, such as the Lambton, Hetton & Joicey Colliery, the distinction between the two types of railway was blurred, with privately owned locomotives and stock having the rare permission to run over parts of the national network.

The Lambton Colliery railway system dates back nearly three centuries to the opening of a waggonway between Fatfield and Cox Green in 1737, with early steam locomotives introduced around 1814.

In 1819, J G Lambton, who later became the Earl of Lambton, bought the Newbottle

waggonway, a 5¾ mile concern which linked mines to deep water berthing at Sunderland, and linked it to the Lambton waggonway with a new line between Burnmoor and Philadelphia near Houghton-le-Spring, affording his coal wagons direct access to the River Wear at Sunderland. This new route was worked by stationary engines until the mid-1860s.

After the North Eastern Railway opened its branch from Penshaw on the Leamside line to Sunderland via Cox Green and Pallion in 1865, close to the Lambton network, and a branch from Pallion to Deptford Wharf on the Wear, close to Lambton Staithes, the same year, an agreement was drawn up between the NER and the Lambton Railway.

It granted permission for Lambton Railway locomotives to run over the NER between Penshaw and Lambton Staithes and later to

Sunderland South Dock, and a series of 0-6-0 locomotives was ordered for the purpose.

By the early 20th century, this fleet was becoming outdated for long-haul coal trains from the collieries to the coast, so the Lambton Railway looked to the successful 0-6-2 tank engines being used for heavy coal traffic in the South Wales valleys.

In 1904, an 0-6-2T was bought from Kitson & Co of Leeds and it became the railway's No. 29. Another six of the type followed, from different manufacturers, between then and 1934. They included No. 5, built in 1909 by Robert Stephenson at Darlington.

In 1911, the Lambton system took over the Hetton Railway and built a tunnel bypassing its rope inclines to give steam locomotives access to its northern reaches including Hetton Staithes for the first time.

Lambton, Hetton & Joicey Colliery No. 5 heads the North Riding County Council special on July 23, 1971. JOHN BOYES/W J ARMSTRONG TRUST

In 1924, the Joicey collieries were added to this particular empire, becoming the Lambton Hetton & Joicey Colliery.

With the decline of the Durham coalfield the Hetton Railway via Warden Law was eventually closed in 1959, followed by Lambton Staithes in January 1967 and the line to Pallion in August that same year, ending hauling over the national network by the company's locomotives.

Steam locomotive working on the Lambton system ended in February 1969 and its last section, between Lambton Coke works and Penshaw, closed in January 1986.

Both Nos. 5 and 29 are now part of the North Yorkshire Moors Railway collection.

They came under scrutiny in 1969 when the embryonic heritage line was seeking locomotives, and an offer by enthusiast groups – including Chris Cubitt, a former engine cleaner at Thornaby depot – to buy them was accepted the following year.

On June 19, 1970, No. 29 was steamed and British Rail gave permission for it to be towed in steam to Grosmont on June 25, with NER T2 0-8-0 No. 2238. They immediately made their debut between Goathland and Grosmont during a gala weekend.

No. 5 followed that August, first being painted with NYMR letters at Thornaby and then moved to the North Yorkshire Moors Railway on the 28th of that month.

Along with the T2, it headed all of the passenger trains during the August Bank Holiday weekend steam gala which immediately followed its arrival.

Both became popular engines on the NYMR and a trademark of the line. No. 29 returned to steam in 2013 after its latest overhaul while No. 5 is awaiting restoration.

LNER J27 0-6-0 NO. 65894

The embryonic years of the railway preservation movement saw societies formed not only to save closed lines but also to preserve locomotives that were otherwise destined for the scrapyard.

In 1966, the North Eastern Locomotive Preservation Group, a charity run by volunteers, was formed with the aim of preserving some of the steam locomotives still working in the region. Within 18 months, NELPG had raised sufficient money to buy two heavy freight locomotives in the form of J27 0-6-0 No. 65894 and Q6 0-8-0 No. 63395.

Both were overhauled and transferred to the NYMR in the early Seventies.

The acquisitions were followed in 1972 by mixed-traffic K1 2-6-0 No. 62005 which was donated to the group. Seven years later, the group was offered Q7 0-8-0 No. 63460 – another heavy freight locomotive – on long-term loan by the National Railway Museum in York, and in 1983, bought J72 0-6-0T No. 69023 *Joem*.

In late 1987, the group took the sole-surviving A2 Pacific No. 60532 *Blue Peter* on long-term loan.

NELPG's aim is not merely to save locomotives and place them on display in museums, but to have as many of its steam locomotives running as possible.

Its main workshop is at Hopetown Carriage Works in Darlington although it also has a workshop and base at Grosmont.

No. 65894 is typical of a workaday locomotive that was an everyday sight in the North East, right up until the closing years of steam.

Classified P3 by the NER, it was designed by Wilson Worsdell as a minor modification of the existing P2. Indeed, the P3s were the largest NER 0-6-0s.

The first 80 were built between 1906-09 in five batches by Darlington Works, North British, Beyer Peacock, and Robert Stephenson. A further batch of 25 were built at Darlington with Schmidt superheaters and piston valves and delivered in 1921-22.

These were followed by a final order of 10 placed in December 1922 and built by the LNER at Darlington. Reclassified J27 by the LNER in 1926, the superheated J27s could be identified by their extended smokeboxes.

After the Second World War, the J27s were mainly used for hauling heavy mineral trains. The first withdrawals came in March 1959, but in June 1966, 36 were still giving sterling service, hauling coal in County Durham and South Northumberland.

The last ones were withdrawn from the Blyth area where they operated the short trip workings between the nearby coalfield and shipping staithes, finally finishing in September 1967. A remarkable record for a type which started out in the Edwardian era.

Built at Darlington in 1923 as No. 2392, the J27 was allocated to Bank Top shed, Darlington, before moving to Ferryhill to cover Durham coalfield workings until reallocated in 1930 to York. From there, it mainly saw use on local goods trains to Scarborough. In 1946, under the LNER's renumbering scheme, No. 2392 became No. 5894. After nationalisation in 1948, the engine was renumbered again as No. 65894.

No. 65894 spent most of its British Railways career at York. In 1963, during a visit to Darlington Works, it was fitted with a non-superheated boiler.

On October 2, 1966, the engine was transferred to Sunderland South Dock where ➤

Not only did P3 0-6-0 No. 2392 haul the opening train on the NYMR, but carried out a similar function on the Weardale Railway on July 17, 2004. It is seen bringing the reopening train into Stanhope ready for the 11.15am departure to Wolsingham on July 17, 2004. BRIAN SHARPE

it joined the other surviving J27s working coal trains in East Durham. September 9, 1967, saw it work the last diagrammed steam turn from Sunderland shed.

Withdrawal along with the four other survivors swiftly followed and No. 65894 was sent to Tyne Dock for disposal where it was bought directly from British Rail on December 1, 1967 after a long hard fundraising campaign. At first stored at Tyne Dock where restoration began, it was returned to steam professionally at the then still functioning National Coal Board workshops at Philadelphia in County Durham, first moving under its own power in the heritage era in December 1968.

Despite British Rail's post-August 1967 steam haulage ban, the J27 moved under its own power via Newcastle Central station to Thornaby shed on April 11, 1969, where restoration work continued.

The fitting of vacuum brake and steam heating apparatus for working passenger trains, along with other final tasks were undertaken by the group's volunteers at ICI Billingham.

Resplendent in NER lined black livery, the locomotive moved to the NYMR on October 23 1971, where it entered service the following weekend hauling members' trains on occasional open days and was chosen to haul the NYMR's official reopening train carrying the Duchess of Kent.

The P3 has been a popular locomotive in the heritage sector, taking part in the Rail 150 Stockton & Darlington cavalcade at Shildon in 1975, and visiting several other lines.

From 1977-82 it was on static display in the National Railway Museum in York. A further overhaul preceded its return to NYMR traffic in autumn 1984.

After another overhaul at ICI Wilton, it returned to the NYMR in May 1996 in British Railways' livery as No. 65894, hauling its comeback train on June 6 that year.

In 1998, it gained a certificate to run on the main line, at the time the only NYMR-based engine allowed to do so.

Accordingly, it ran two return trips between Grosmont and Whitby, marking what

would become, as we will see, be the start of what a regular service of steam specials on the Esk Valley line.

In June 2003, it reverted to NER livery and renumbered 2392 for the last five years of its boiler certificate.

It had the honour of being the opening train on a second northern line, that of the Weardale Railway in 2004.

The failure of a repair to a fracture in the cylinder casting led to the J27 spending the final year of its boiler ticket at the Locomotion museum at Shildon.

Its few days in steam saw it run on the demonstration track at Head of Steam, the Darlington railway museum, where it took part in the Darlington North Road 40th anniversary celebrations in June 2006.

While it has been a solid and popular performer on the NYMR, it can haul only seven coaches up the 1-in-49 gradients, and so in the peak summer periods has been loaned out to other lines. It is now under overhaul in Darlington.

WD AUSTERITY 2-10-0 NO. 3672 *DAME VERA LYNN*

We saw earlier how Britain's railways were starved of investment during the years of wartime austerity. However, locomotive building had to continue in earnest, as the time would come when they would be needed on a continent where the Nazis and their allies were being pushed back.

The War Department commissioned several Austerity steam locomotive types. They were labelled as such because while they were very powerful locomotives, they

were also no-frills types, a diametric contrast to the glamorous streamliners of the LNER and LMS of the Thirties. They were designed to go anywhere, and needing the bare minimum of maintenance to keep costs and turnaround time down.

One WD Austerity type was the 2-10-0 designed by Robert Riddles, the wartime director of transportation equipment, who at nationalisation became a member of the Railway Executive for Mechanical and

Electrical Engineering and oversaw the design and production of the 12 British Railways Standard classes.

The 150 Austerity 2-10-0s were based on Riddles' Austerity 2-8-0, and were designed to have interchangeable parts, again to speed up repairs and overhauls. They had the same power output as the 2-8-0 but a lighter axle load making them suitable for secondary lines.

They were the first 2-10-0s to work in

WD Austerity 2-10-0 Dame Vera Lynn when it first arrived on the Lavender Line.

WD Austerity 2-10-0 No. 3672 *Dame Vera Lynn* passes Green End on May 27, 1996. DAVID IDLE/NYMR

Britain, and paved the way for the later British Railways 9F 2-10-0s, regarded by many as the best of the Standard classes.

WD No. 73672 was built in 1944 by the North British Locomotive Works in Glasgow, and after D-Day was shipped to Egypt. It then spent 30 years working in Greece.

In 1984, a party of officials from the Mid Hants Railway arrived at Thessalonica in Greece to purchase from the Hellenic State Railways a US Army Transportation Corps S160 2-8-0 and two WD Austerity 2-10-0s.

One of them went to the Lavender Line in East Sussex, where it was named *Dame Vera Lynn* in 1986, while the other two worked on the Mid Hants.

Eventually, *Dame Vera Lynn* moved to the NYMR and entered traffic in 1989. Over the next decade it clocked up more than 100,000 miles in traffic, but its boiler ticket ran out in 1998, leaving it to await its place in the overhaul queue.

Still waiting in 2014, a £750,000 nationwide appeal was launched to pay for its overhaul

under the banner of the Fight for Vera Fund, with the aim of having it back in steam by 2019, its 75th anniversary.

The Fight for Vera Fund would also like to see the locomotive become a national memorial to the people from the Austerity years who built it during a time of international hardship.

Another member of the class which was once based on the NYMR, No. 90775, was sold by owning group the Essex Locomotive Society to the North Norfolk Railway in 2005.

THREE S15s MAKE TWO GOOD ONES

The S15 4-6-0 freight locomotive was designed for the LSWR by locomotive superintendent Robert W Urie, based on his H15 class and N15 class locomotives. They first appeared in 1920, and were the last of a class which eventually numbered 45 in 1936, in Southern Railway days. The last to work under British Railways was withdrawn in 1966.

Urie's successor Richard Maunsell revised the cylinder arrangement of the S15s, allowing a second batch to be built, again at Eastleigh Works, followed by a third batch in 1931.

The S15s were regarded by locomotive crews as an excellent goods engine best known for working heavy night express goods trains between Exeter, Southampton and Nine Elms. The S15s were also very capable passenger engines, being able to deputise in situations where there was a shortage of passenger locomotives during peak holiday periods.

Seven survived into preservation, three being owned by the Essex Locomotive Society and now based on the NYMR.

I say 'based' loosely, because these three survive only on paper.

No. 841 was built in July 1936 and after withdrawal in January 1964, arrived at the legendary Dai Woodham's Barry scrapyard that June.

At some stage, Dai Woodham decided to stop cutting up locomotives sent by British Railways for the time being, and concentrate on the more immediately profitable scrapping of mineral wagons.

Accordingly, lines of rusting locomotives, mainly from the Southern and Western regions, were amassed at the scrapyard. His decision, unique among scrapmen, gave the preservation movement time to mature to the point where it was able to buy the scrap locomotives for restoration.

A total of 213 were saved for preservation purposes – I choose those words carefully, because not all of these would be restored in their own right. Some would be cannibalised for spares to restore other locomotives.

No. 30841 became the 24th locomotive to be bought from Barry scrapyard. Moved by the Essex Locomotive Society to the East Anglian

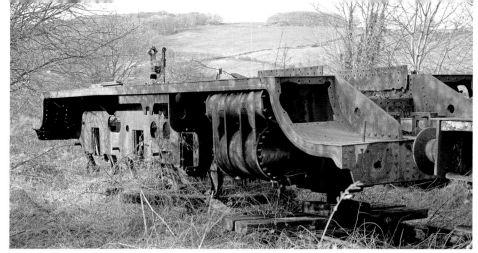

The twisted frames of S15 4-6-0 No. 841. BRIAN SHARPE

Railway Museum at Chappel & Wakes Colne on September 23, 1972, it returned to steam in 1974, in Southern Railway livery, carrying the name *Greene King*, a local brewery having sponsored the restoration.

In August 1975, SR No. 841 after restoration, travelled under its own steam from Essex to the Stockton & Darlington Railway 150th anniversary celebrations at Shildon.

In 1976-77, efforts were made to run No. 841 on the main line in East Anglia, but it failed on several occasions, the last being in October 1977.

No. 841 was towed to the Nene Valley Railway where it was repaired and worked service trains. Its owning group soon decided to relocate to the NYMR, where No. 841 arrived under its own steam on December 9, 1978.

Built in 1927, sister No. 825 is the oldest-surviving Southern Railway-built S15. Withdrawn in January 1964, it arrived at Barry five months later.

Unlike other Barry rescues, No. 30825 left the scrapyard in two parts. The boiler went to the Mid Hants Railway in 1981 and was fitted to Urie S15 No. 30506.

The frames – the single component of a locomotive which gives it an identity – and the wheels went to the workshops of Steam & Sail Ltd at Brightlingsea, Essex, in November 1986. It was intended to build a new all-welded boiler and restore the locomotive, but after this venture failed, the remains of the engine were acquired by the Essex Loco Society in 1990.

After several years in traffic, NYMR shed staff found that No. 841, a useful member of the

operating fleet for many years, had twisted and cracked frames. They were replaced by those from No. 825, the hybrid engine taking the identity of the latter in line with tradition.

No. 841 is likely to donate further parts to the eventual restoration of No. 830, which dated from 1927 and, withdrawn in July 1964, arrived at Barry that December.

The last Southern engine left in the scrapyard, it was bought by Maunsell Locomotive Society member David Jones as a source of spares for the society's No. 847 in September 1987 and was moved to the Bluebell Railway.

At one stage there was talk of converting it to a King Arthur 4-6-0, but in 1996 it was bought by the society. It was later decided that the group did not have the resources to restore it, and so what was by then left – the frames, cylinders wheelsets and a boiler in poor condition – was sold to the Essex Locomotive Society – on condition that it will be restored in its own right.

The components are now stored on the NYMR. The long-term plan is to use the remains of No. 841 as a source of spares for No. 830.

The boiler has to be tackled first, and placed on No. 825 so that it can be fast-tracked back into service. A new tender will be needed for No. 830 as it did not have one when it left Barry. An ex-SR snowplough built on a six-wheel tender chassis has been acquired for that purpose – although most S15s ran with eight wheeled bogie tenders some did run with six-wheel tenders.

BELOW: S15 4-6-0 No. 825 passes Moorgates with the 'Moorlander' dining train on December 10 2011. DAVID WARREN

GWR 0-6-2T NO. 6619

Following the Grouping of 1923, the GWR inherited a motley collection of 0-6-2Ts from the companies serving the South Wales valleys which were expected to haul heavy coal traffic.

The pre-Grouping tanks were showing their age, but they were very powerful, for their size, with a high adhesive weight and good braking ability and were popular with their crews.

They were designed to run only short distances, mainly from the collieries to harbours such as Cardiff and Barry, as well as branch passenger trains, and so did not need high capacity water tanks or large bunkers.

The GWR looked at these attributes and then using the Rhymney Railway M and R classes as a starting point designed two new series of 0-6-2Ts, which emerged as the 56XX and 66XX classes.

Withdrawn from traffic between 1962-65, nine survived into preservation, including No. 6619 which was built at Swindon in January 1928 and withdrawn in February 1963. Its front end suffered minor damage when it became derailed – while shunting scrap locomotives in Barry scrapyard.

In October 1974, it became the 64th locomotive to leave Barry scrapyard. It was taken to the NYMR and extensively rebuilt between 1979 and 1984, with some input from Kent & East Sussex Railway volunteers.

On the NYMR, No. 6619 was a popular and economical engine easily capable of working eight coach trains over the gradients.

Following its last overhaul, it has visited other heritage lines. In November 2012, it was sold by owners Kevin Gould and Peter Proud to a consortium from the Kent & East Sussex Railway and it is now in service there.

The total mileage run by No. 6619 since its first steaming on October 7, 1984, until November 6, 2012, when it left the NYMR, was 90,494.

GWR 0-6-2T No. 6619 begins the 1-in-49 climb to Goathland on February 10, 2005.
BRIAN SHARPE

SCHOOLS CLASS 4-4-0 NO. 30926 *REPTON*

The most powerful 4-4-0 locomotives ever to run in Britain, the Schools class first made an appearance on the Southern Railway in 1930.

No. 30926 *Repton* was built at Eastleigh in May 1934, and entered service on the Bournemouth route, also operating between Waterloo and Portsmouth before that line was electrified.

Repton was one of the last of the class to be overhauled by British Railways in 1960, and therefore was considered a good choice for preservation after withdrawal in December 1962. Spending several years in storage, it returned to Eastleigh Works in April 1966 and was externally restored and outshopped on February 28, 1967 – not for a return to the main line, but for export to North America, after being bought by a US enthusiast.

Along with London & South Western Railway M7 0-4-4T No. 30053, it was shipped to Montreal in Canada on board the SS *Roonagh Head* from Gladstone Dock, Liverpool, in April 1967.

Repton was donated by the purchaser to Steamtown, USA in Vermont. It was displayed at the museum at Bellows Falls from November 1967 and was loaned to the Cape Breton Steam Railway in Canada. However, it became neglected while there, and an offer was made by British enthusiasts to bring both locomotives back home.

They were repatriated to the UK, arriving at Brightlingsea on April 10, 1989. Found to be in good condition, *Repton* was restored on the NYMR where it was used regularly before being loaned to the Great Central Railway from 1991-93. No. 30053 has enjoyed a second life on the Swanage Railway.

Repton last came out of service in 2010 for a boiler overhaul.

LMS 'BLACK FIVE' NO. 45428 *ERIC TREACY*

One of several preserved members of this go-anywhere/do-anything extremely versatile class of mixed-traffic locomotive, Stanier 'Black Five' No.45428 was built as LMS No. 5428 in 1937 by Armstrong Whitworth at Scotswood Works in Newcastle-on-Tyne.

Part of an order for 227 locomotives, the largest order ever placed with a private firm, it became a member of a class which eventually numbered 842.

It was bought privately for preservation in October 1967, and was first kept at Tyseley in Birmingham, where the steam depot was being slowly transformed into a preservation base.

In 1969, it was named after the famous railway photographer and author Eric Treacy, who was Bishop of Wakefield.

Bishop Eric Treacy pictured after a wedding at Christ Church in Halifax in 1971. RJ STOTT*

No. 30926 *Repton* approaches Glaisdale on a NYMR Esk Valley line service from Whitby on March 7, 2010. DEE DAVISION

No. 45428 was moved to the NYMR in November 1973. On August 31, 2010, after returning to traffic following an overhaul.

Born in London, Eric Treacy was educated at Haberdashers' Aske's School and at King's College. He began taking photographs shortly after joining the clergy in 1932, and three years later joined the Railway Photographic Society.

During the Second World War he became an army padre, for which he was later made an MBE.

His first book of railway photography was published in 1946. He became rector of Keighley and in 1949 was appointed archdeacon of Halifax.

In 1961 he became suffragan bishop of Pontefract and in 1968 was made Bishop of Wakefield, holding the post until he retired in 1976.

On May 13, 1978, he was waiting at Appleby station on the Settle and Carlisle line to photograph a railtour hauled by BR Standard 9F No. 92220 Evening Star, when he died from a heart attack.

A slate plaque is displayed on the main station building to his memory. He is buried at St Kentigern's Church, Crosthwaite, Keswick.

The Treacy Collection of 12,000 photographs forms part of the National Railway Museum's archive of more than 1.4 million images.

Photographed from Carwath bridge, LMS 'Black Five' No. 45428 Eric Treacy prepares to depart Goathland en route to Pickering with the Pullman dining train on September 28, 2013. PHILIP BENHAM

BULLEID REBUILT WEST COUNTRY LIGHT PACIFIC NO. 34101 *HARTLAND*

While Sir Nigel Gresley introduced his A4 streamlined Pacifics to the LNER, it was his assistant, Oliver Bulleid, who designed 4-6-2s with air-smoothed casings for the Southern Railway, after taking over there as chief mechanical engineer.

No. 34101 Hartland was one of only six Bulleid light Pacifics to be built at Eastleigh Works, being outshopped in February 1950. It was rebuilt at Eastleigh in September 1960, when as in the case of many other Bulleid Pacifics, the streamlined casing was removed in order to reduce maintenance costs. Withdrawn in July 1966, it arrived at Barry in October 1966.

Richard Shaw of Shaws Metals Ltd purchased it and in July 1978, it became the 92nd locomotive to leave Dai Woodham's

scrapyard when Shaw moved it to his engineering works at Sinfin in Derby for restoration, with the aid of members of the Hartland Preservation Society.

Partially restored, Hartland was moved to the Great Central Railway on March 18, 1991. Restoration was completed at Loughborough in late 1993, and No. 34101 entered traffic in January 1994. Its official launch was held on April 30, 1994.

The locomotive had been destined for the Peak Rail Matlock to Buxton revival. It moved to Peak Rail at Matlock in May 1995 and spent a few months in service there before moving to the NYMR, where it was in regular service until withdrawal for overhaul in 2000.

It is due to re-enter traffic in 2015.

West Country light Pacific No. 34101 Hartland with A2 No. 60532 Blue Peter at Grosmont during the NYMR's Rail 175 gala on October 6-8, 2000. ROBIN JONES

LMS 'BLACK FIVE' NO. 44767 *GEORGE STEPHENSON*

No. 44767 is unique out of all the 'Black Fives', and its name gives a clue as to the reason why.

In 1947, Stanier's successor, H G Ivatt, built 30 'Black Fives' to different designs to take into account modern developments to reduce maintenance, such as manganese axlebox liners, rocking fire grates, self-emptying hopper ashpans, self-cleaning smokebox and continuous boiler blow down, with the aim of testing them against the standard model.

Six locomotives were fitted with double chimneys and electric headlights. One of them, No. 4767 was not fitted with the standard Walschaerts valve gear, but for the first time in a century, an experimental set of outside Stephenson valve gear.

Out of the 30 experimental 'Black Fives' developed for Ivatt's trials, only No. 4767 – outshopped from Crewe on December 31, 1947, the last day of the LMS – has survived.

Renumbered No. 44767 at nationalisation, it was withdrawn from Carlisle Kingmoor on New Year's Eve 1967, a day after the shed closed, and exactly 20 years since it entered traffic.

It was one of those saved through the efforts of the late Morecambe GP Dr Peter Beet, who in the dying days of British Railways' main line steam tried to find buyers for the remaining 'Black Fives', and who helped set up the Steamtown museum at Carnforth depot.

The tender of No. 44767 was scrapped by mistake at Carlisle, but the locomotive remained intact.

Dr Beet persuaded the late Brian Hollingsworth to buy No. 44767 for £2100. It was then coupled to a tender which came from the experimental fleet of 30 but which had been latterly attached to sister No. 44950.

At Steamtown, the restoration of No. 44767 began slowly. In 1972, it was agreed to have it restored by Hunslet, moved to Grosmont and then officially named Duchess of Kent when she opened the line on May 1, 1973. It never happened because the contractual agreements could not be made and the restoration was not completed in time.

The same year, local councils in the North East were making plans to stage a locomotive cavalcade to mark the 150th anniversary of the Stockton and Darlington Railway in 1975.

NYMR general manager the late John Bellwood wanted to move No. 44767 from Carnforth to Grosmont, and wondered if the event organisers might cover the cost if it appeared in the cavalcade.

In return, it was suggested that Brian Hollingsworth name his locomotive after George Stephenson, celebrating both his work on the Stockton & Darlington and his invention of the link motion which No. 44767 uniquely carried.

The local authorities agreed to pay for the movement and a set of brass nameplates, and NELPG agreed to restore the locomotive at Thornaby. In January 1975, Brian sold the engine to the then NELPG chairman Ian Storey.

No. 44767 steamed for the first time in preservation on March 15, 1975.

On August 25 that year, at a 150th anniversary exhibition in Shildon, the nameplates were unveiled by the son of general manager of the LNER, William Whitelaw, and it took part in the Grand Cavalcade six days later, watched by 350,000 people as it led a procession of NELPG's four restored engines.

Afterwards, it was based on the NYMR, and on July 4, 1976, returned to main line service, hauling the Newcastle to Stockton leg of 'The Scarborough Flyer'. Afterwards, it became a regular performer on the national network.

Following the completion of its last overhaul in 2009, it has run on the Great Central, Churnet Valley and West Somerset railways, and Ian has since based it on the North Norfolk Railway.

LMS 'Black Five' 4-6-0 No. 44767 prepares to head the 4.30pm train from Goathland to Pickering on May 8, 2011. PHILIP BENHAM

LNER K1 2-6-0 No. 62005 passes beneath Larpool viaduct with the 2.15pm Whitby to Pickering service on October 23, 2007. BRIAN SHARPE

LNER K1 2-6-0 NO. 62005 *LORD OF THE ISLES*

Although the sole-surviving K1, No. 62005, was not built until 1949 – a year after nationalisation – the ancestry of its design dates back to the Great Northern Railway.

The last LNER chief mechanical engineer, Arthur H Peppercorn, is credited with the design, but the groundwork was done by Nigel Gresley at the GNR.

Gresley's first locomotive design was influenced by the popularity of the 2-6-0 wheel arrangement in North America. The result was the GNR class H2, which later became the LNER's original class K1.

That type developed into the K2s, which excelled in particular on the West Highland Line. However, Gresley wanted a more powerful 2-6-0 type for this route, and so developed his three-cylinder K4s, of which only six were built.

After Gresley's death in 1941, Edward Thompson became chief mechanical engineer and modified K4 No. 3445 into a two-cylinder design.

Peppercorn further modified the design and ordered a batch of 70 from the North British Locomotive Company, all of which were delivered after nationalisation.

As all of the original LNER K1s had been converted to K2s by 1937, this new type took over the K1 classification with the prototype being K1/1. All of the class were fitted with a BTH speedometer and electric lighting powered by a Stones steam turbine.

Further modifications in BR days included fitting an automatic warning system to some locomotives, including No. 62005.

First shedded at Darlington after running in at Eastfield shed in Glasgow, No. 62005 was based at Heaton, Darlington, Ardsley, York, North Blyth and Tyne Dock before it was finally allocated to Holbeck in September 1967.

It was condemned on December 30, 1967, and sold to a consortium of Viscount Garnock,

Geoff Drury, Brian Hollingsworth and George Nissen in May 30, 1969.

They did not intend to restore the locomotive, but merely wanted its boiler as a spare for K4 No. 61994 *The Great Marquess*, which they had bought, and which as LNER No. 3442 worked the special on the last day of the Whitby to Scarborough and Malton to Pickering lines.

No. 62005 survived into 1969 only because it had been used for a brief period as a temporary stationary boiler at ICI's North Tees works at Seal Sands on Teesside.

However, once purchased, the boiler was not needed for the K4, so the K1 was donated to NELPG in 1972 and was delivered to Thornaby on June 14 that year.

There it was overhauled by volunteers and in accordance with the wishes of the donating group, was painted in a fully lined LNER green livery. Restored, it arrived at the NYMR in late May 1974 and entered traffic on June 8.

In 1975 it made its first heritage-era main line runs on the Esk Valley line between Whitby and Battersby before joining the Stockton & Darlington cavalcade at Shildon that August. It also ran on the main line on several occasions in the late Seventies.

June 28, 1987, saw the K1 begin a long association with the West Highland Extension from Fort William to Mallaig, hauling special trains, at first for British Rail, and later for the West Coast Railway Company, operators of the phenomenally successful summer 'Jacobite' daily steam trips. Indeed, in 1994, it attended the West Highland Railway centenary celebrations, and was paired with the K4, for which it had been bought as a donor locomotive!

The locomotive was named *Lord of the Isles* in preservation.

Withdrawn for overhaul in 1994, the K1 returned to traffic in 1998, again hauling main line tours. In 2005, the K1 worked a special to celebrate the 40th anniversary of the closure of the Whitby to Pickering route. The choice of the K1 was appropriate because it had, along with the K4, run the last special under British Railways in 1965.

Following another major overhaul in 2007, it re-entered service on the NYMR, but nowadays spends much time away from the line, because of its commitments elsewhere, notably on the West Highland Extension.

BELOW: K1 2-6-0 No. 62005 passes Ellerbeck on April 9, 2007. PHILIP BENHAM

BR STANDARD 4MT 2-6-0 NO. 75029 *THE GREEN KNIGHT*

In the last days of British Railways steam, there were several private individuals as well as embryonic heritage lines who were determined to do all that they could to save locomotives for future generations.

Among them was David Shepherd, now far better known across the globe as a painter and wildlife conservationist than for his pioneering work in railway preservation. He used the proceeds from a sell-out exhibition of his early wildlife paintings in New York to buy not one but two engines – firstly BR Standard 4MT 2-6-0 No. 75029, which he later named *The Green Knight*, and BR Standard 9F 2-10-0 No. 92203, which he named *Black Prince*.

Following the purchases in 1967, the pair were moved to Crewe South while David looked for a permanent home for the pair, and chose the Longmoor Military Railway. The two engines duly moved south over the weekend of April 6-7, 1968, double heading for most of the way.

The engines were steamed occasionally at Longmoor and took part in open days. However, the scheme spearheaded by David to preserve a section of this famous MoD line failed to take off and when it closed, the preserved stock that had been based there had to be found new homes.

David's two engines took up temporary residence at Eastleigh Works, while he negotiated the purchase of a length of former

BR line on which they could be run. A total of 31 locations in the south of England were considered including the Meon Valley route in Hampshire, Radstock, the pre-preservation Swanage branch and the Hayling Island branch.

However, he eventually managed to secure a section of the redundant GWR Cheddar Valley route based on Cranmore station, after an appeal to acquire the whole section leading from there into Shepton Mallet failed through lack of public financial support.

At Cranmore, David built a two-road GWR-style brick engine shed in which to keep his locomotives. By late 1973, the site was ready for the engines, and the movement took place on November 18 that year. No. 75029 ran there via the main line, hauling a selection of passenger stock which had been collected for use on the nascent East Somerset Railway as the line was to be known.

David spent much of the next two decades building up the East Somerset, with *The Green Knight* and *Black Prince* as its flagship locomotives, but eventually reduced his involvement and then pulled out of active involvement so he could concentrate on his international wildlife campaigns.

The Green Knight was sold to NYMR chairman Pete Best in 1998, initially on a long-term hire deal and later purchased outright, to pay for the overhaul of *Black Prince*.

It was restored to steam on the NYMR in

2000 but was withdrawn for further work in 2003.

When Pete Best decided to sell it in 2005, the NYMR beat off rival bids from Dart Valley Railway plc, the West Coast Railway Company and Bury engineer Ian Riley with help from a benefactor. Following a major overhaul at Grosmont in 2011, it returned to service.

Designed by Robert Riddles, the class was introduced in 1951. They were intended for mixed-traffic use on secondary routes where the BR Standard 5MTs and their predecessors, the LMS 'Black Fives', were too heavy. They were basically a tender version of the BR Standard 4MT 2-6-4Ts, with similar characteristics to the GWR Manor 4-6-0s, but unlike the Manors were built to the universal loading gauge.

Built at Swindon in 1954, No. 75029's British Railways career saw it work mostly on the Western Region, its initial allocation being Laira. Afterwards it was shedded at Oxford (twice), Gloucester, Southport, Swindon, Tyseley, Machynlleth, Croes Newydd (twice), Llandudno Junction, Shrewsbury, and finally Stoke (June 1967), from where it was withdrawn in August 1967.

BR Standard 4MT 2-6-0 No. 75029 heads along the northern bank of the River Esk towards Larpool viaduct en route to Whitby.
PHILIP BENHAM

BR Standard 4MT 2-6-0 No. 76079 departs from Whitby on June 8, 2011. STUART BROWN

BR STANDARD 4MT 2-6-0 NO. 76079

Robert Riddles' BR Standard 4MT 2-6-0s were designed at Doncaster Works, which built 25 of the 115-strong class, and intended mainly for freight working.

Built at Horwich Works in February 1957, No. 76079 was first allocated to Sutton Oak, and on June 24, 1967, it was posted to the Wigan Springs branch, where it was withdrawn in December that year.

Bought by enthusiast Derek Foster, it left Barry in July 1974 and initially became a static exhibit at the now-closed Steamport museum in Southport.

In 1986, it was moved to a private site in

Liverpool for restoration, and returned to steam in 1989. From there, it was moved to the East Lancashire Railway where it ran in traffic until it was transferred to the Llangollen Railway in August 1992. It returned to the East Lancashire on November 26, 1998, when it was bought by Bury engineer Ian Riley.

He first steamed it in May 2001, and it joined his other operational locomotives on the main line.

By then a frequent visitor to the NYMR, the 'Pocket Rocket' was sold to the heritage line by Ian on August 27, 2009, with eight years left on its boiler ticket. The NYMR trust board

decided that the cost of buying the locomotive would be roughly equal to that of overhauling one of its stored engines.

The locomotive was later removed from service for a boiler mid-life overhaul and for the repair and replacement of its cracked right cylinder. The crack was known about and a replacement cylinder was already under construction at Grosmont, ready for the day when it would be needed.

The boiler was steam tested in July 2014 paving the way for reassembly to begin with – at time of going to press – an expected return to service in September 2014.

BR STANDARD 4MT 2-6-4T NO. 80135

One of 15 surviving examples of this extremely useful, powerful and very versatile Riddles Standard tank, No. 80135 was built at Brighton Works in April 1956 and was first allocated to Plaistow shed for use on the London, Tilbury & Southend lines.

It was later based at Tilbury, Shrewsbury (twice) and Oswestry. One of its first enthusiast-oriented assignments came in June 1957 when it hauled the Railway Enthusiasts' Club's 'London Suburban' tour to North Woolwich, Chingford, Cheshunt and Hereford. Withdrawn from Shrewsbury in July 1965, it arrived at Barry scrapyard the following January.

In April 1973, it became the 39th locomotive to leave Woodham Brothers' yard when it was purchased by the NYMR and moved to Pickering, representative of a type which regularly worked over the line from Whitby to Pickering and York.

It was later sold to Dutch enthusiast Jos de Crau, who funded its initial restoration to working order and owned it for many years but it was later purchased back by the railway. No. 80135 at one stage became the highest mileage engine on the NYMR. Indeed, No. 80135 and WD 2-10-0 No. 3672 *Dame Vera Lynn* became the first two steam locomotives to break the 100,000-mile barrier in preservation.

A popular locomotive, it last steamed in November 2007, after which a £350,000 overhaul was required. The NYMR's £1 million Bridges &

Wheels Appeal, launched in 2009 to raise funds for the replacement of Bridge 30, as covered in a later chapter, also included the overhaul of No. 80135 as the 'Wheels' element. The

overhaul includes an all-new copper firebox fabricated in-house at Grosmont to replace an all-steel version which proved less than successful.

No. 80135's sister locomotive No. 80072, hired by the NYMR to cover for its absence, arrives at Levisham on May 5, 2012. PHILIP BENHAM

'BLACK FIVE' 4-6-0 NO. 44806 *MAGPIE* FLIES ITS NEST

The latest 'Black Five' to run on the North Yorkshire Moors Railway is also its newest locomotive acquisition, No. 44806.

Built at Derby in July 1944 as LMS No. 4806, it was first allocated to Saltley, and was then shedded at Kentish Town, Nottingham, Burton, Speke Junction and Lostock Hall, from where it was withdrawn in August 1968, the last month of British Rail steam haulage.

It was among the group of 'Black Fives' that the aforementioned Dr Peter Beet strove to save with the aid of friends and contacts. No. 44806, its post-nationalisation number, was bought by enthusiast Ken Aldcroft straight from BR service and first moved to the Steamtown museum at Carnforth, later moving to the Lakeside & Haverthwaite Railway on November 26, 1970.

In 1973, while it was based at Haverthwaite, it was adopted by ITV's children's hour series Magpie and named after the show – a response to the BBC's comparable Blue Peter show, which had earlier adopted LNER A2 Pacific No. 60532 *Blue Peter*. It ran in green livery for a time.

However, a crack was found in the outer firebox, and Haverthwaite did not have the workshop facilities to tackle it. No. 44806 was moved to Steamport in Southport in 1975.

The repair was not undertaken, and in 1983, No. 44806 was moved to the Museum of Science and Industry in Manchester as a static exhibit.

In February 1993, *Magpie* flew on to the Llangollen Railway where repairs finally began. It returned to steam on September 15, 1995, initially as No. 4806 in black LMS livery with red lining, then again as No. 44806 in BR livery.

Ken Aldcroft died in 2003. No. 44806 passed to his daughter Renee Wyatt. To mark his 35 years of ownership, 10 years longer than it had been in LMS and BR service combined, it was renamed *Kenneth Aldcroft*.

Following another overhaul, the locomotive returned to steam on August 29, 2007, in BR unlined black.

It has never been loaned to other railways and is unique among the six one-time Carnforth 'Black Fives' in never having run on the main line in preservation.

However, in 2013, Renee Wyatt placed it on the market. The successful bidder was a rich supporter of the NYMR, who bought it and promptly donated it to the NYMR Historical Trust.

Following a farewell gala at Llangollen on January 4-5, 2014, it was moved to its new home. Llangollen Railway spokesman George Jones said: "No. 44806 has been a firm favourite with steam fans throughout its stay with us. It has been a reliable workhorse and will be much missed."

As one of the later 'Black Fives' it has a higher superheat boiler than Grosmont-based sister No. 45428 *Eric Treacy* and may therefore have slightly better performance.

Newly-arrived 'Black Five' No. 44806 passes Beck Hole with the 12.44pm Grosmont-Pickering 'local' on May 3, 2014. PHILIP BENHAM

B1 4-6-0 NO. 61264

Britain's heritage steam fleet shows a distinct bias towards Southern and Great Western types, for the simple reason that they comprised the bulk of the locomotives sent to Barry scrapyard, where a stay of execution was given by owner Dai Woodham for commercial reasons.

Elsewhere, locomotives were cut up within days of arrival in a breaker's yard: there was no similarly benevolent scrapman elsewhere, and so the LNER and especially the Scottish Region fared badly in the preservation stakes, with many classes of steam locomotive being rendered extinct overnight.

One LNER locomotive, however, was saved from Barry – Edward Thompson B1 4-6-0 No. 61264, which in July 1976 became the 83rd steam engine to be sold by the yard.

A total of 410 B1s were built between 1942 and 1952.

Built by North British in Glasgow in December 1947, the locomotive was first allocated to Parkston shed in Essex, and worked the heavy Harwich to Liverpool Street 'Scandinavian' boat trains.

In November 1960, as a result of the introduction of electric trains and diesel locomotives on the Great Eastern section, No. 61264 was switched to Colwick depot near Nottingham.

From there, it was used on express passenger services between Nottingham,

J72 0-6-0T NO. 69023 *JOEM*

The smallest of the NELPG steam fleet but by no means any the less popular for it is J72 0-6-0T No. 69023 *Joem*.

The J72 class is remarkable in that it was designed by William Worsdell for the NER with the first examples appearing as the E1 class in 1898, yet they were still being built by British Railways in 1952.

The first batch of 20 engines was built at Darlington North Road Works in 1899. The NER built a further 55 engines from 1914 to 1922.

Nigel Gresley reclassified the engines as J72s and built 10 at Doncaster in 1925. British Railways built a further batch at Darlington, 20 in 1949 and eight in 1951, bringing the total to 113. The last batch were nearly identical to the originals but had a vacuum brake, steam heating and sanding gear to allow them to be used on empty passenger stock workings.

They were also used in shunting yards, docks and coal staithes and on station pilot workings all over the North East. Again somewhat remarkably, all 113 remained in service until 1958, when they began to be replaced by diesel shunters.

Only two had not been scrapped by 1964. These were Nos. 69005 and 69023, which were taken into Departmental Stock as No. 58 and No. 59 and used at North Blyth and Heaton for de-icing. No. 69005 was scrapped but No. 69023 became the only survivor when it was purchased by Ronald Ainsworth for preservation, and moved from Holbeck shed to the Keighley & Worth Valley Railway on October 16, 1966.

Leicester and Marylebone along the old Great Central route.

No. 61264 was withdrawn from Colwick in November 1965. It was then transferred to Departmental stock as No. 29 and used as a stationary boiler at Colwick until July 1967.

Following its purchase, it moved to the Great Central Railway where it was reunited with the other surviving B1, No. 1306.

Initially there were fears that the boiler and firebox of No. 61264 were so beyond repair that the locomotive might have been sent back to Barry, but eventually, specialists at Pridham Engineering of Tavistock managed to carry out the necessary repairs.

Owned by the Thompson B1 Locomotive Trust, No. 61264 returned to steam on March 6, 1997, ending a 20-year restoration.

For the next decade, it ran extensively on both the main line and several heritage railways. In May 1998, No. 61264 starred in London Underground's popular Steam on the Met event, and it worked its first 'Jacobite' trains on the West Highland extension the following year.

Withdrawn in 2008 for a heavy general overhaul, having run over 80,000 miles, nearly

£500,000 has been spent on repairing and renewing No. 61264's boiler, all funded by donations and loans from supporters.

The boiler was rebuilt at Pete Waterman's LNWR Works in Crewe and the job involved a new inner firebox, smokebox, smokebox door, tubes, front and back tubeplates, stays, outer firebox sides, the ashpan, throatplate, and a third of the firebox outer backplate.

It returned to steam to give public train

rides in the yard at Crewe on October 27, 2012.

With the overhaul finally completed in December 2012, No. 61264 was moved to its new long-term home on the North Yorkshire Moors Railway, entering traffic on March 2, 2013. It is now a mainstay of the locomotive roster.

In 2014, it ran in the guise of scrapped sister No. 61034 Chiru, a veteran of the lines around Whitby.

LNER B1 4-6-0 No. 61264, running as No. 61002 *Impala*, departs from Whitby on May 6 2013. No. 61002 is thought to be the last B1 to work over the line prior to closure. BRIAN SHARPE

Three days earlier, in the middle of the night, it was driven down the East Coast Main Line through Newcastle, Durham, Darlington, York and on to the shed. It was the longest journey that the little engine would ever have made, and British Railways staff had even made up a wooden extension to the coal rails to increase the capacity.

At Keighley, it was professionally repainted in NER livery, and named *Joem*. The key to the name was once carried on a small brass plate on the cabside which read: "This locomotive, Joem, is preserved in memory of Joseph S Ainsworth (50 years LNWR), and his wife Emmeline, by their son Ronald".

On the KWVR, *Joem* was used on Santa specials and other duties between 1968 and 1970, and featured in the BBC TV version of The Railway Children which preceded the EMI box office version.

It was sold in 1977 to the Derwent Valley Light Railway at York. There, after several years of inactivity, it was retubed and used to start a new steam passenger service on this private (but not preserved) line.

It was even passed for main line running for scenes in Harrogate station in the film Agatha starring Dustin Hoffman and Vanessa Redgrave.

However, the Derwent Valley Light Railway, which had been built for carrying agricultural produce, wanted to close the line and sell off the land for development. The former owner's son, Paul Ainsworth, exercised the family's option to buy back the J72 and moved it to the National Railway Museum for storage prior to sale.

It was offered for sale by Sotherby's in London on December 4, 1981, but failed to reach the reserve price of £25,000. It seemed that heritage railways were deterred by its limited haulage capacity.

NELPG officials then met Paul Ainsworth and negotiated the sale price down to £10,250. The sale was completed on November 20, 1982, after which it moved to the NYMR in January 1983 and was steamed within four months.

In September 1984, the NYMR found itself with no other working engines apart from *Joem*. The little engine was left to work the only passenger service which comprised two round trips from Grosmont to Pickering.

Withdrawn from traffic in late 1985, *Joem* was overhauled at ICI Wilton and repainting into NER/BR pattern-lined green was undertaken. Afterwards it returned to the NYMR and was used on regular lightweight trains as well as Grosmont station pilot. It has visited many other railways.

Its boiler ticket expired in 1996 but it did not reach the head of the restoration queue until 2004, when it was moved from Grosmont to NELPG's workshop at Darlington for an extensive £150,000 overhaul completed with the aid of a £50,000 grant from the Heritage Lottery Fund.

It ran again on the NYMR in 2012 following the completion of its overhaul, but because of its diminutive size and limited usefulness on a line which has heavy loadings at peak periods, NELPG has hired it out to other railways. In 2014, it spent the summer season on loan to the Wensleydale Railway.

NER J72 0-6-0T No. 69023 *Joem* and Lambton Colliery 0-6-2T No. 5 climb past Beck Hole on October 11 1987. BRIAN SHARPE

LMS 'BLACK FIVES' NOS. 44871 AND 45407

Not part of the line's permanent steam fleet, you might be forgiven for thinking that Bury engineer Ian Riley's main line certified 'Black Fives' are NYMR locomotives by the back door!

They have visited the line each year on loan for the best part of the past decade in between their railtour commitments on the national network.

No. 4871 emerged from Crewe Works on March 31, 1945. Based at Longsight at nationalisation, if was officially withdrawn from Carnforth on August 31, 1968, three weeks after the last main line steam train under British Railways ran.

Indeed, it was one of the two 'Black Fives' that worked the 'Fifteen Guinea Special' south from Carlisle on August 11, 1968.

Thanks to the machinations of Dr Peter Beet, it was immediately bought for preservation at the Steamtown museum being set up at Carnforth and remained there, working railtours after 1972-73 including 'Jacobite' trips over the West Highland extension in the 1980s.

It was sold to a new owner who moved it to the Bo'ness & Kinneil Railway on July 14, 1990. It acquired the name *Sovereign* and worked regularly on the main line including Aberdeen-Inverness trains, until purchased by Ian on September 20, 2006.

It returned to steam two years later following the fitting of modern equipment for running over the national network including Automatic Warning System, Train Protection & Warning System and On-Train Monitoring & Recording apparatus and air brakes.

No. 5407 was built by the Armstrong Whitworth in Newcastle in 1937 and first based at Kettering, ending up at Lostock Hall in 1968.

Although thanks to the best efforts of Beet,

LMS 'Black Five' No. 44871 passes Moorgates on March 18, 2012. PHILIP BENHAM

the locomotive was purchased by David Davis for £3300 and was subsequently moved to Carnforth for restoration, carrying Furness Railway red livery for a while.

In 1974 it was bought by Paddy Smith who operated the engine on the main line, including the Settle & Carlisle, Cumbrian Coast and Crewe to Holyhead routes, in LMS livery as No. 5407. However, it became best known for its exploits on the West Highland Extension, where it spent three seasons in the late Eighties.

After the last season in Scotland, it was moved to Carnforth for new tyres. Afterwards, it was based on the East Lancashire Railway and visited other heritage lines during the last

three years of its boiler ticket.

Paddy sold the engine to Ian Riley in 1997. It was overhauled at Bury, and given a new tender tank with greater water capacity and fitted with air brakes and AWS apparatus.

It became even more regular on the main line back in BR livery as 45407, though it ran for a while as No. 45157 *The Glasgow Highlander*, after one of only four out of 842 'Black Fives' to carry names in the steam era.

Now named *The Lancashire Fusilier*, No. 45407 is one of the most widely travelled and consistently reliable engines on the main line, regularly hauling West Coast Railways' 'Jacobite' between Fort William and Mallaig.

A2 PACIFIC NO. 60532 *BLUE PETER*

An illustrious performer sadly missed from NYMR metals in recent years is the only surviving Peppercorn A2 Pacific, No. 60532 *Blue Peter*.

Built at Doncaster Works and outshopped in LNER apple green on March 25, 1948, it followed the LNER tradition of naming locomotives after famous racehorses.

Blue Peter III was the name of a horse owned by Harry Primrose, 6th Earl of Rosebery, which in 1939 won races including the Epsom Derby and the 2000 Guineas.

No. 60532 was allocated to York, from where it worked principally over the East Coast Main Line.

In autumn 1949, five A2s including No. 60532 were modified at Doncaster, receiving a multiple valve regulator and a double blastpipe and chimney, together with Kylchap cowls. No. 60532 received a second whistle placed offside behind the chimney.

Afterwards, all five were moved to Scotland and No. 60532 was allocated to Aberdeen, from where it was mainly used on express passenger services to Edinburgh. Later reallocated to Dundee, No. 60532 became the last Peppercorn Pacific to be overhauled at Darlington Works.

In the dying days of steam, it became a popular choice to head railtours, working to Exeter and Holyhead. It was withdrawn on New Year's Eve 1966.

It was subsequently bought by enthusiast Geoff Drury, who had already purchased LNER A4 No. 4464 Bittern from British Rail in 1966. He tried to buy an A1, but after the last one was cut up he was offered No. 60532 in 1968.

It became adopted by the BBC TV programme Blue Peter, and once restored, was repainted in LNER apple green livery as No. 532. At a Doncaster Works Open Day in 1971, 60,000 people witnessed its renaming by the Blue Peter presenters.

It was moved to the now-closed Dinting Railway Centre at Glossop in Derbyshire, but saw scant use, and in late 1987 the NELPG took charge of both No. 60532 and A4 *Bittern* on long-term loan from the Drury family. It was restored at ICI Wilton and again renamed by the Blue Peter programme in December 1991.

Blue Peter was then moved to the NYMR for running in. The following year, it gained its main line certificate and worked many railtours, including several over the Settle and

Carlisle line and some as far north as its old home of Aberdeen.

However, in 1994, during the first run of a preserved steam locomotive from Edinburgh to Newcastle, *Blue Peter* suffered extensive damage during an uncontrolled wheelslip.

Repairs to the damaged motion, cylinders and driving wheels at Thornaby depot took 18 months. Again, No. 60532 returned to the NYMR for running in.

It was back on the national network in November 1996, working a charter from Middlesbrough to Preston, and in 1998 No. 60532 ran an Edinburgh to London excursion to mark the 40th anniversary of its TV programme namesake.

Again based at the NYMR, its main line boiler certificate expired in September 2001. It worked on the heritage line until the end of the 2002 season before going on static display at the Head of Steam museum in Darlington. In 2007, it moved to Barrow Hill Roundhouse and has been there on static display ever since. NELPG needs to raise £600,000 to restore it for main line running.

The locomotive is still owned by the Drury family, who have resisted offers to sell it.

NER Q7 0-8-0 No. 901 at Grosmont on October 3, 1993. BRIAN SHARPE

NER T3 0-8-0 NO. 901

Designed by Sir Vincent Raven and originally classified as NER T3, No. 901 was the first of the class of 0-8-0s to be built. They were the most powerful freight locomotives built by the NER.

No. 901 was outshopped from North Road in September 1919, and excelled in load-hauling trials between Perth and Edinburgh. First allocated to Blaydon, it was transferred to Hull Dairycoates in December 1923, and used to haul coal trains between the South Yorkshire pits and Hull Docks. By 1929 it was back in the North East, shedded at Haverton Hill, Stockton, West Hartlepool and Darlington.

During the Second World War, all 15 class members were shedded at Tyne Dock, later

working the heavy Consett iron ore-trains, after being equipped with vacuum brake equipment and two Westinghouse pumps for opening and closing the air-operated doors on the ore wagons. It was only the mighty BR Standard 9F 2-10-0s that ousted them from this job.

The class became Q7s in 1926, and in 1946 No. 901 was renumbered 3460. After nationalisation in 1948 it became No. 63460. As such it stayed at Tyne Dock until it was withdrawn on December 3, 1962.

Preserved as part of the National Collection, it headed railtours in the North East in 1963 and 1964.

In 1979 the National Railway Museum, where it had arrived the previous year,

and NELP reached an agreement under which the group would restore it. Moved to the NYMR, the overhaul began at Grosmont in 1982.

Nine years later, the Q7 entered traffic on the line in LNER livery. It became a popular and regular performer which had no trouble with heavy peak season loadings.

Withdrawn in 1999, it remained in store in NELPG's Deviation shed at Grosmont until June 2004 when it was moved by road to Shildon. There, it became the first steam locomotive to arrive at Locomotion, the National Railway Museum's new outreach museum. It is now on display in the Head of Steam museum at Darlington's North Road station.

A2 Peppercorn Pacific No. 60532 *Blue Peter* passes Water Ark on a NYMR service train. BRIAN SHARPE

SOMERSET & DORSET 7F 2-8-0 NO. 53809

A popular performer on the NYMR, but never formally based on the line, was Somerset & Dorset Joint Railway 7F 2-8-0 No. 53809.

Built to a Midland Railway design by the Darlington Works of Robert Stephenson & Co in 1925, it hauled heavy freight trains from Bath Green Park to Templecombe. It was rebuilt by the LMS in 1929 following a runaway accident which left three railway staff in Bath goods yard dead.

In the Fifties, the type was used to haul summer holiday expresses over the Mendip hills between Bath and Bournemouth.

Withdrawn in June 1964, it arrived at Barry scrapyard in August 1964. It was purchased in 1975 by NYMR supporter Frank Beaumont for use on the line.

However, he did not live to see the completion of restoration work on his engine, most of which was carried out at a private non-rail connected site at Kirk Smeaton in South Yorkshire.

Moved to what is now known as the Midland Railway-Butterley, it was rapidly restored to main line standard by 1980, just in time for it to take part in the Rainhill 150 celebrations to mark the 150th anniversary of the opening of the Liverpool & Manchester Railway, and enjoyed an eventful main line career in the Eighties and Nineties.

It has remained Butterley based ever since, but in late 2005, it was announced that it would be going on loan to the NYMR for an indefinite stay following completion of its latest overhaul.

It ran in traffic until 2011, when it was taken back to Butterley for repairs. Still there at the time of writing, the NYMR would be delighted to have it back, after several successful seasons of running it.

Somerset & Dorset Joint Railway 7F 2-8-0 No. 53809 arrives at Pickering – before the trainshed roof was replaced – with the LNER teak coach set. PHILIP BENHAM

GWR 2-8-0T NO. 5224

Owned by pop mogul Pete Waterman, Churchward heavy freight 2-8-0T No. 5224 has been based at the NYMR on loan, and has since been hired to other heritage lines.

Introduced in 1901, the purpose of the class was working the 1000 tonne coal trains up through the South Wales valleys, a job which required much tractive effort and good steaming capabilities. These qualities served No. 5224 well on the NYMR,

Outshopped from Swindon in May 1924, No. 5224 was first allocated to Newport.

It was withdrawn from Cardiff East Docks in April 1963 and reached Barry scrapyard four months later.

Bought for preservation in October 1978, it moved to the Great Central railway and was returned to steam at Loughborough in October 1984.

GWR 2-8-0T No. 5224 heads past Darnholm with the LNER teak set on October 1, 2005. BRIAN SHARPE

BR STANDARD 9F 2-10-0 NO. 92214

One of the shortest NYMR locomotive careers was that of BR Standard 9F 2-10-0 No. 92214.

Built at Swindon in October 1959, as one of the last steam locomotives constructed by British Railways, and a veteran of the Somerset & Dorset line summer holiday traffic as well as the Banbury to South Wales ironstone traffic, it was withdrawn in October 1965. The fact that it had just six years' service highlighted the sheer wastefulness in areas of British Railways during the changeover from steam to diesel.

It was bought from Barry scrapyard for preservation in December 1980, moving at first to Peak Rail's original site at Buxton. It was eventually restored to running order at the Midland Railway-Butterley by the 9F Locomotive Charitable Trust

No. 92214 was hired by the NYMR and arrived in 2010. However, it was very quickly bought from the trust by Grosmont company PV Premier Ltd, which is headed by Stuart Whitter, one of the railway's volunteer drivers.

On April 22, 2011, it was officially named *Cock o' The North* prior to the departure of the 10.30am from Grosmont.

The name was suggested by Valerie Walter, company secretary of PV Premier Ltd, and whose grandfather served with the Gordon Highlanders during the First World War. Cock O' The North is the traditional epithet attached to the chief of the Gordon clan, and reflects the historic power of the Highland clans. The name was also carried by the first of Nigel Gresley P2 2-8-2s, No. 2001, which appeared in 1934. The first locomotive to bear the name was a North British Atlantic which changed its name to *Aberdonian* when the P2 appeared, and more recently, Class 87 electric locomotive No. 87022 carried it.

At Grosmont, No. 92214 underwent a fast-track 10-year boiler overhaul during 2012-13.

It later visited the Great Central Railway for its January 24-26, 2014, winter steam gala – and did not return to Pickering.

GCR director Michael Gregory of Cromwell Tools bought the locomotive from PV Premier Ltd, and added it to the Loughborough fleet permanently. GCR managing director Bill Ford said: "No. 92214 is a magnificent addition to the GCR's already impressive locomotive fleet and being in such immaculate condition will prove a great attraction to our many visitors.

"On behalf of the railway we would like to thank Stuart for the very professional way in which the transaction has been completed."

Four months later, No. 92214 was painted in BR Brunswick green livery, the only other 9F to have carried it being No. 92220 *Evening Star*, because of its special status as the last British Railways' steam locomotive built.

The new *Cock 'o The North* passes Water Ark on May 5, 2012. PHILIP BENHAM

LMS 'BLACK FIVE' 4-6-0 NO. 45212

The last British Railways' steam locomotive in regular service is held to be 'Black Five' 4-6-0 No. 45212.

Based at Preston's Lostock Hall shed, the locomotive, built by Armstrong Whitworth in 1935, operated the last scheduled steam train on August 4, 1968, British Rail's official Last Day of Steam.

The Keighley & Worth Valley Railway bought the locomotive directly from British Railways in 1969 and it was in regular use until withdrawn for a major overhaul in the mid-1970s.

It came to the NYMR on an extended loan deal arranged between the KWVR and NYMR supporter Peter Best around 2000, in which the line would have the use of the locomotive.

Since having returned to Keighley, No. 45212 is now subject to a 10-year agreement with Bury-based engineer Ian Riley, under which it will undergo a major overhaul which will allow it to head main line specials and will spend three months per year on the KWVR as well as visiting other heritage lines.

Severely cold conditions beset Britain just before Christmas 2010. Some trains were cancelled or ran late because of severe frost with the maximum daytime temperature being minus 10°C. LMS 'Black Five' No. 45212 is seen heading light engine past Moorgates en route to Pickering.
DAVE COLLIER

THE DIESEL FLEET

The NYMR has a diesel fleet which not only acts as backup in times of locomotive failure or dry summers when there is a risk of lineside fires, but which haul passenger trains in their own right.

Class 24 D5032 was built at Crewe and entered traffic at March in July 1959. After a spell at Stratford the following year, it moved to Willesden and then to Bletchley in 1961. It was withdrawn from Crewe Diesel Depot as No. 24032, on July 17, 1976, and sold to Stockton scrap dealer T J Thomson Ltd a week later.

However, the NYMR obtained it on long-term loan, and by 1986 had covered 100,000 miles in preservation. It was named *Helen Turner* after the daughter of a director of the scrap dealer.

The second Class 24 to move to the NYMR was Crewe-built D5061, which entered London Midland Region traffic on January 15, 1960. It was withdrawn from Crewe on August 10, 1975. That October, it became Departmental stock as No. TDB968007 at Derby Works.

Withdrawn a second time on December 18, 1978, it was given a new lease of life with the Railway Technical Centre at Derby. There it was renumbered as 97201 on August 18, 1979, named *Experiment* the following June and withdrawn for a third time on December 4, 1987, moving to Vic Berry's Leicester scrapyard under its own power in July 1988.

It was purchased for heritage use and moved to the Midland Railway-Butterly on July 19, 1991. After a brief spell on the North Tyneside Railway, it arrived at the NYMR, where its first duty on this railway was as the star of a KitKat advertisement.

It was overhauled and repainted into early British Railway green livery minus the yellow warning panel. It later became the permanent way department's locomotive.

Class 25 D7628 was built by Beyer Peacock in Manchester as one of the last of a batch of 26, entering service at Tinsley in October 1965. Under the TOPS scheme, it was renumbered 25278.

The last of its class to receive a general overhaul, at Derby in 1981, it was withdrawn on March 15, 1987, yet called back into service to haul a Bescot to Crewe freight two days later.

Painted in a two-tone green livery and named Sybilla, at the request of its then owner and longstanding Dutch NYMR benefactor Jos De Crau, in 1998 it gained RESCO certification for limited use on the Esk Valley line.

Privately owned dual-braked Class 37 No. 37264, built at Vulcan Foundry in 1965, and originally numbered D6964, was withdrawn by British Rail in December 1999. It is currently operational, and carries BR large logo blue livery.

Class 37 No. 37264 departs from Grosmont on June 13, 2014. ROBIN JONES

USATC 2-8-0 NO. 2253

In 1942, while plans were being drawn up for an invasion of Nazi-occupied Europe, the Allies realised the need for heavy freight locomotives with easy maintenance and maximum route availability. Two basic designs were produced: the Riddles Austerities, like No. 3672 *Dame Vera Lynn*, and the American S160s.

The S160s were designed by a committee of engineers from three American firms, to a specification set by the Ministry of Supply. The first of more than 800 (out of more than 2100 built) arrived in the UK in 1942 and production continued until 1947.

No. 2253 was outshopped by the Baldwin Locomotive Company in May 1943. Once over here, it was modified for British working, with vacuum brakes fitted.

Along with 167 other S160s, it was allocated to the LNER and posted to Neville Hill shed in Leeds. From there, it may have worked over the Malton-Whitby line.

Shipped to liberated France in September 1944, it was subsequently sold on as part of the Marshall Plan to Polish State Railways, where it became No. Tr 203.208. It was finally withdrawn in 1985 and placed in storage at Olesnica, near Wroclaw.

NYMR staff heard of it and went to investigate. Peter Best agreed buy the locomotive and fund its restoration.

Its overhaul completed, it was sent by road to England via a North Sea crossing from Gdynia to Teesport. It arrived at New Bridge yard in Pickering on October 29, 1992, just in time to haul freight trains during the NYMR's wartime weekend.

It ran on the NYMR for seven years, covering 41,000 miles before boiler issues stopped the engine. Afterwards, it was laid up in a siding for many years. In 2013, the NYMR decided to have a clear-out of unwanted and surplus stock, with the threat that it could be scrapped if no interest was shown.

In late 2013, it was bought – for the second time – by Pete Best's Steam Powered Services Ltd. A condition of sale was that it was removed from the NYMR for restoration.

Agreement was reached for it to go on display cosmetically restored at the Locomotion museum in Shildon, from June 2014 until September 2015, as an example of the US Army locomotives built in preparation for the D-Day landings on June 6, 1944.

Inside Locomotion's main building, No. 2253 is displayed as a wartime train with the museum's own warflat wagon and Crusader tank. It is not known whether, once returned to steam, it may return to the NYMR.

USATC S160 2-8-0 No. 2253 on static display inside the Locomotion museum in Shildon in May 2014. LOCOMOTION

Above: LMS 'Black Five' 4-6-0 No. 45428 calls at Aidensfield (Goathland) station with a rake of British Railways' maroon and cream Mk.1 coaches. NYMR

HEARTBEAT

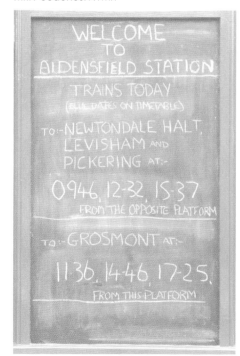

Notice of services from Aidensfield. NYMR

The silver screen has always been a great bedfellow for the heritage railway movement.

The 1953 British comedy film The Titfield Thunderbolt revolves around a group of villagers trying to keep their branch line operating after British Railways decides to close it.

The film, released eight years before anyone in railways had heard of Dr Richard Beeching, was written by Thomas Ernest Bennett 'Tibby' Clarke, who was inspired by the restoration of the Talyllyn Railway.

Starring Stanley Holloway, George Relph and John Gregson, it was the first Ealing comedy shot in Technicolor and one of the first colour comedies made in the UK.

Clarke drew much inspiration from Talyllyn saviour L T C Rolt's book Railway Adventure which had been published the year before. Several scenes in the film, such as the emergency resupply of water to the locomotive by buckets from an adjacent stream, or passengers being asked to assist in pushing the carriages, were borrowed from the book.

The Titfield Thunderbolt has been credited with giving an enormous boost to the newborn volunteer-led heritage railway movement. Back in 1950, when Rolt assembled his team to take over the ailing obscure railway in mid-Wales, there must have been those who wondered why. At the time, there was no serious threat to steam traction: British Railways was yet to turn out 999 Standard locomotives before modernisation won the day. Saving a line using an everyday form of traction would be like preserving a commonplace Vauxhall Astra: today you are an eccentric – but tomorrow you are a visionary.

Still, the film was a huge box office hit and made the public aware of the dawn of the preservation movement and its basic concept.

Fast forward another 17 years, and EMI filmed its big-screen version of Edith A Nesbit's seminal children's classic The Railway Children starring the red knickers-waving Jenny Agutter, Sally Thomsett and Bernard Cribbins on the Keighley & Worth Valley Railway.

At a time when railway preservation was still in its comparative infancy, the railway made the film, and the film made the railway. An enormous

Claude Greengrass (Bill Maynard). NYMR

Trains to Goathland station are still packed with visitors eager to see sets from Heartbeat, including Aidensfield Garage. ROBIN JONES

Shops in Goathland still do a roaring trade in Heartbeat souvenirs. ROBIN JONES

Waiting for a train at Aidensfield. NYMR

Film crews set up at Goathland (Aidensfield) station. NYMR

PC Mike Bradley, played by Jason Durr, with one of the locomotive crews. NYMR

success, it is still hailed as one of the most influential children's films of all time.

The phenomenal amount of publicity that it generated for the heritage railway, which had then been open for just two years, ensured that even decades later, crowds still flock to it, wanting to see the now-legendary filming locations.

Another massive hit, this time on the small screen, similarly 'made' the North Yorkshire Moors Railway for millions more.

TV first aired the Sixties police drama series Heartbeat on Friday, April 10, 1992.

Made by ITV studios, formerly Yorkshire Television, in its first year of transmission Heartbeat averaged 14.5 million viewers and was often in the top five TV programmes in the

UK as far as audience figures were concerned.

Originally based around a motorcycle-riding village police constable, Nick Rowan, played by EastEnders actor Nick Berry, it had Sixties pop music as a background linking the scenes. Berry also sung the theme song, a cover of Buddy Holly's classic Heartbeat. However, a centrepiece was the railway, which featured in most episodes. It was also the focal point of several episodes, with a train crash, a stolen bullion van and criminal chases along the tracks as storylines.

The village of Goathland became Aidensfield, and trains were seen bringing characters to the station and taking them away again.

Never mind that occasionally some of the songs were hits after the end of British Railways

PC Mike Bradley, Oscar Blaketon, Nurse Maggie Bolton, Alf Ventress, Gina Ward and PC Bellamy wave goodbye to Nick, Joe and Katie Rowan as they depart from Aidensfield station for a new life in Canada. REX FEATURES

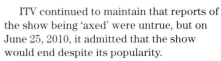

steam in August 1968, such as The Hollies' 1974 hit The Air That I Breathe, or the fact that the line in real life had closed before many were even recorded. Aidensfield was all but a fantasy setting loosely based on a village in the moors, filled with many semi-rustic characters such as Claude Greengrass (Bill Maynard), with Brow House Farm near Goathland doubling up as his home.

The public loved it, and were switched on to the railway big time too.

Awesome scenery, a superb locomotive fleet, those wonderful teak carriages – they all contributed to making the NYMR Britain's most popular heritage line.

However, there are many who affirm that it was Heartbeat that provided the catalyst to send it soaring to the top of the charts and kept it there year after year.

Many characters came and went over the years. Derek Fowlds, who played police sergeant turned pub owner Oscar Blaketon and William Simons, who took the role of PC Alf Ventress, were the only main-cast actors who remained with the show over its entire 18 series run.

The series was often repeated during the summer, giving the railway much-needed peak-season publicity.

"TV FIRST AIRED THE SIXTIES POLICE DRAMA SERIES HEARTBEAT ON FRIDAY, APRIL 10, 1992. "

On January 28, 2009, it was announced that the production of both Heartbeat and its spin-off show The Royal would be suspended for an unspecified period of time so that a large backlog of unbroadcast episodes could be cleared.

Newspaper reports subsequently claimed that the shows had been ditched owing to budgetary constraints in the light of falling advertising revenues, at a time the worst recession in decades was biting hard.

ITV bosses contacted Heartbeat cast and crew members to discuss the future of the show in March 2009. It was revealed that they would be released from their contracts after the end of series 18, meaning that the show had been permanently cancelled.

There was uproar, not only from Heartbeat fans around the world but also from moorland communities which had built up a brisk trade from the hordes of tourists.

ITV continued to maintain that reports of the show being 'axed' were untrue, but on June 25, 2010, it admitted that the show would end despite its popularity.

A spokesman said: "Heartbeat has been an important part of the television landscape over the last 18 years and we are incredibly proud of what it achieved in its heyday as one of ITV1's top-rated dramas."

The final series was filmed from May 2008 to May 2009, with the last and 372nd episode screened on September 12, 2010, in Britain.

Over the years it had collected three ITV Programme of the Year awards, and in 1999 it was named Best Performing Peak-Time Drama, with ratings higher than Coronation Street and Who Wants To Be A Millionaire.

The show has been screen in Australia, Belgium, Canada, Denmark, Estonia, Finland, Ireland, the Netherlands, New Zealand, Sweden and Lithuania. In 2007, Norwegian

Above: A police car from the TV series on display in Goathland. ROBIN JONES

Left: The Goathland Hotel became the Aidensfield Arms in the TV series. ROBIN JONES

Right: Stop in the name of the law: PC Phil Bellamy and Sergeant George Miller bring a train to a standstill. REX FEATURES

PC Rob Walker chases villains who stole freight trucks with a rogue locomotive. REX FEATURES

viewers voted it Best European Drama.

However, from a peak of 15.82 million viewers for series seven in 1997-1998, audiences had fallen off to 5.44 million by 2010.

In recent times it has been shown again on ITV3. Who knows – maybe, like Dr Who, Heartbeat may one day be successfully revived and be an even bigger hit than before.

If that happens, the producer will already have a complete set of perfect filming locations, and a splendid steam railway that more than fits the Old Bill! ■

On a wintry day the Aidensfield bobby chats to the crew of Southern Railway Schools class 4-4-0 No. 30926 *Repton*, a long way off its Southern Region home territory. REX FEATURES

CHAPTER 11

The triple triumph

The reopening of the Grosmont to Pickering line is itself an against-the-odds success. However, the North Yorkshire Moors Railway did not rest on its laurels, but went on to aim even higher.

Uniquely among standard gauge heritage lines, it went on to 'acquire' a second and adjacent route 'by the back door', in the form of running power over Network Rail's Esk Valley line, which it joins at Grosmont.

Finally, the ultimate triumph has been not only running regular services from Pickering to George Stephenson's original terminus of Whitby via the Esk Valley line, but also having

its own platform built at Whitby station.

For the best part of its first four decades, the NYMR was known as the railway that went from Pickering to Grosmont and no further. Yet from the hills above Grosmont the coast and seaside resort of Whitby could easily and tantalisingly be seen, and indeed, from the earliest days of preservation there were those who maintained hopes that one day it would be possible for trains to run between Pickering and Whitby once again.

As early as 1987, the NYMR ran special trains through to Whitby using the services of British Rail and the National Railway

Museum's historic BR Standard 9F 2-10-0 No. 92220 *Evening Star*, which in 1960 had become the last main line steam locomotive built for use in the UK by British Railways. These trips marked the start of occasional trains on the Esk Valley line.

On November 22, 2000, the NYMR ran its debut 'Captain Cook Pullman' steam-hauled dining train from Pickering to Whitby, with all 308 seats selling out within just three days of going on sale.

The excursion was hauled by the North Eastern Locomotive Preservation Group's NER J27 class 0-6-0 No. 65894, and used the NYMR's

'Moorlander' carriage set, which had been passed for main line running, including Metropolitan Cammell Pullman cars *Robin* and *Opal*.

Following privatisation, the West Coast Railway Company operated the trains using NYMR locomotives and carriages until 2003. The condition of the track over the last 10 miles to Whitby then caused Network Rail to halt such operations.

Following major track renewals over the next two years, helped by the intervention of then-Whitby MP Lawrie Quinn, himself a railwayman, it became possible to resume locomotive operations in 2005, just in time to allow a special Pullman train on March 4 commemorating the 40th anniversary of the line's closure, headed by K1 2-6-0 No. 62005.

However, privatisation had changed the rules of the game; in principle, anyone who could demonstrate they were a fit body to run a safe and reliable service could apply to operate over Network Rail.

The prospect of regular steam back into Whitby now seemed much more likely. However, there were well-meaning doubters who said that regular steam to Whitby just could not be done.

They claimed that the cost of running over even a short stretch of Network Rail would be prohibitive, and would jeopardise the financial wellbeing of Grosmont to Pickering, the core business. The costs just don't stack up, they added.

The doubters also said that running a second steam railway so near to the first would merely take away business, robbing Peter to pay Paul while doubling the costs. They also suggested that people travel to the NYMR for the magnificent upland scenery, which is largely absent on the Esk Valley line, and so nobody would be interested in riding over it. Who on earth would want to travel to what is left of Battersby Junction in the middle of nowhere? Network Rail would never allow volunteer crews. They hadn't got the experience. And so on...

However, the decision was made to go for it.

The first step was to test the market, and a series of pilot operations took place in the summers of 2005 and 2006, with trains again being operated by West Coast between Whitby, Grosmont and Glaisdale. However, the limited facilities at Grosmont made it impracticable to run trains regularly between the two networks, with passengers having to change trains at Grosmont.

History was made between September 29 and October 1, 2006, with hardly anyone realising it at the time... not even general manager Philip Benham.

Another major milestone: BR Standard 4MT 4-6-0 No. 75029 *The Green Knight* approaches Whitby on April 6, 2007, with the first public timetabled North Yorkshire Moors Railway-operated steam train to the resort. DAVE RODGERS

CHANGE FOR WHITBY TOWN & MIDDLESBROUGH

GROSMONT

In 2004, Philip Benham, who at one time was British Rail's area manager for York and then King's Cross, took a sideways career move. After spending 18 months as consultant to the Strategic Rail Authority, he entered the preservation sector and took what many believe to be the top job, superseding Peter Pay as general manager of the NYMR. There, the question he faced was 'what can you do to make the best line better?' And the answer? In 2007, the NYMR won the Heritage Railway Association's Annual Award, at a time when it was both celebrating its 40th anniversary and running timetabled services on the Esk Valley line. Third from left, he is seen celebrating the award along with a party of North Yorkshire Moors Railway officials, staff and volunteers at Pickering. ROBIN JONES

The 8.45am 'early bird' service on Saturday, normally a DMU trip from Pickering to Grosmont, was upgraded not only to steam, but also to a through train to Whitby.

It inadvertently became the first timetabled steam service to run along the whole length of George Stephenson's Whitby and Pickering Railway since it was closed in 1965.

The significance of the trip was lost as bumper crowds, lured by the sight of LNER A4 Pacific No 60007 *Sir Nigel Gresley* coupled to its rake of teak coaches, flocked to the gala to ride on more than 100 trains.

The honour of hauling the 'first' scheduled heritage-era service over the whole of the historic route went to Lambton Hetton & Joicey Collieries 0-6-2T No. 29. The Kitson industrial tank, however, was not passed for main line running, and so locomotives had to be changed at Grosmont. Ian Riley's BR Standard 4MT 2-6-0 No 76079 took the first timetabled run over the western end of the Esk Valley branch into the port, which was, as mentioned earlier, later sold to the NYMR.

"It was only as an afterthought that we realised the significance of the early bird train," said Philip. "We have run special charters over the line to Whitby before, but none of them were timetabled."

During the event, there were 16 special NYMR trains on the Esk Valley line, interwoven between the normal timetabled DMU trips and hauled by No. 76079. Most of the main line trips were said to be well loaded – some with virtually all seats taken – boding well for the future.

Based on the success of the first of such pilot operations, the landmark decision was made to seek a licence for NYMR to operate its own services over Network Rail, and to become its own train operating company, another first for a UK heritage line, despite its unpaid part-time crews. The NYMR is hopeful of being given a licence to run its own services over the Esk Valley line into Whitby in 2015.

A related issue was the question of access between NYMR and Network Rail at Grosmont.

Ian Riley's LMS 'Black Five' 4-6-0 No. 45407 accelerates the 2.10pm Whitby-Battersby train through Lealholm station on the Esk Valley line on May 1, 2011. MAURICE BURNS

The Esk Valley line from Battersby to Grosmont as depicted on the Ordnance Survey One Inch Tourist Map of 1958.

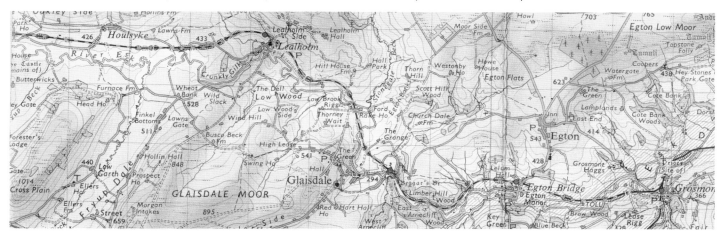

For every train movement, the driver had to be despatched by road to Glaisdale in order to get a single line token out of the signalling instrument there before bringing it back to Grosmont as the authority for the train to proceed on to the Esk Valley single line.

Clearly, this was a cumbersome and time-consuming process, preventing the regular operation of through trains; and a scheme was developed with Network Rail to install an 'intermediate instrument' (which NYMR provided) at Grosmont, allowing a token to be withdrawn and replaced there. In addition to this, to become a licensed train operator on the national network, NYMR had to simultaneously negotiate a Track Access Agreement with Network Rail and satisfy HM Railway Inspectorate, by now part of the Office of Rail Regulation.

The NYMR had to demonstrate that it would be able to operate safely and reliably on the national network. This meant producing and getting accepted a Railway Safety Case (now replaced by a safety certificate). These processes were developed and negotiated throughout 2006. The signing of the Track Access Agreement, which also required ORR approval, and acceptance of the Railway Safety Case both came in February 2007.

On February 13, 2007, No. 62005 headed a route-learning special for train crew over the Esk Valley line, covering the route from Whitby as far west as Battersby – the licence for operations was extended to this location to allow the running of occasional excursions and special trains.

This milestone for the railway was followed by the official launch of NYMR services on Tuesday, April 3, 2007, in a ceremony at Whitby station.

The critics were proved right in one

NYMR locomotive crews at Whitby before undertaking route learning on the Esk Valley line aboard K1 2-6-0 No. 62005 on February 13, 2007. PHILIP BENHAM

respect. The Whitby and Esk Valley services did indeed cause a financial upheaval on the NYMR, but far from making a loss, brought in £125,000 in takings over and above what would normally have been expected during a season.

In that first year of timetabled services, the 'over ambitious' target of 110 Whitby running days was not only met, but also exceeded by 15 additional days.

In the eight years following, the operation of trains between Pickering and Whitby has become a regular feature to the extent that the NYMR can now truly claim to be a railway between Pickering and Whitby.

Nowadays, more than half of NYMR

Watched by Philip Benham and NYMR plc chairman Neal Clarke, the official opening of the timetabled steam services into Whitby was carried out by the Lord Lieutenant of North Yorkshire, Lord Crathorne, on April 3, 2007. NYMR

A rare trip by A4 No. 60007 *Sir Nigel Gresley* from Whitby on May 3, 2008. Because the curves on this section have been deemed two sharp for A4 cartazzi wheelsets, it is highly unlikely that the locomotive will run into Whitby again. PHILIP BENHAM

K1 No. 62005 and a support coach on a route-learning run at Glaisdale on February 13, 2007. PHILIP BENHAM

Another landmark: the first train to be signalled from Grosmont to Whitby with the new Falsgrave gantry was the 9am from Pickering on July 7, 2014. It was topped and tailed by Class 25 D7628 *Sybilla* leading and BR Standard 4MT 4-6-0 No. 75029 at the rear. CRAIG DONALD

passenger ticket income, though not quite yet numbers, arises from travel to and from Whitby.

A significant constraint, however, has been the limited number of train paths available in and out of Whitby. Rationalisation in the 1980s left just a single track and platform at Whitby. Locomotive-hauled trains have had to reverse out of the station to run round in sidings outside the station at Bog Hall. Not only is this very time-consuming, but it also involves propelling trains over a foot level crossing – hardly an ideal situation.

Therefore, early in 2012, the NYMR started negotiations with Network Rail over the possibility of reopening a second platform at Whitby, for which the stub end remained but without any track. These talks continued over the summer period, with a breakthrough being achieved when Network Rail agreed to contribute towards the project if the NYMR could raise the remaining funds. These were to come in the form of a grant from the Coastal Communities Fund, aimed at regeneration and development of coastal areas.

In the event, the cost of the scheme proved to be somewhat higher than first anticipated, finally coming in at around £2.3 million, but still fully funded externally.

The work included reconstruction of the second platform and track with a new alignment and of much greater length than was originally the case.

A third line is also being provided to enable locos to run round in the station. Access is controlled by a new eight-lever ground-frame from the existing single line.

The new layout was commissioned in summer 2014, providing the NYMR with the means to run an enhanced service of five trains in each direction from August that year – an increase of two from the previous three trains in each direction.

An important adjunct to the Whitby scheme has been resignalling work on the railway's own infrastructure at Grosmont to enable trains to and from the Esk Valley to access platform 3 at Grosmont, thus allowing Whitby trains to pass in the station.

The most significant visual element of this project has been the bringing back into use of the former Falsgrave signal gantry from Scarborough. It was the last of its kind on Network Rail when taken out of service in 2011, and a listed structure.

The gantry was recommissioned in early

Falsgrave gantry at its original location in February 2010. CRAIG DONALD

LNER B1 4-6-0 No. 61264 as No. 60134 *Chiru* snakes its way up the Esk Valley line from Whitby on June 13, 2014. More paths on the line are now available following the completion of the Falsgrave gantry at Grosmont, work which was carried out in anticipation of the opening of the North Yorkshire Moors Railway's platform 2 at Whitby on August 2. ROBIN JONES

July 2014, and now controls the passage of trains on to the Esk Valley line, together with access across the whole of the north end of the Grosmont layout. This has been one of the most elaborate signalling schemes undertaken by the small, largely volunteer, but highly professional, NYMR signalling team.

The full benefits from the enhanced Whitby service will be seen in subsequent years and it is anticipated over a three-year period an extra net income per annum of a third of a million pounds will be generated.

Revivalists took a deep breath when urged to go all the way from Grosmont to Pickering from the start. History was repeated when Philip Benham and his team ignored the doubters and led the extension of timetabled steam services to Whitby.

It was a proud day when the new platform 2 was opened in August 2014. Everyone wins.

More visitors to the national park are brought into Whitby, boosting trade without adding to the often nightmarish parking problems. More use is made of the Community Rail Esk Valley line, and those holidaymakers staying in Whitby can access famed beauty spots on the moors.

Furthermore, the port and national park have a world class attraction running through their midst, linking their multi-faceted delights like beads of a necklace. ∎

LMS 'Black Five' No. 45428 departs Whitby with the late-running 2pm service to Pickering on June 25, 2014. The former engine shed is to the left, and the works on the new platform 2 to the right. PHILIP BENHAM

The remodelled trackwork entering the 'new' Whitby platform 2. NIGEL TROTTER

Visiting LNER A4 streamlined Pacific No. 4468 *Bittern* at Battersby with the NYMR's dining train on May 6, 2012. PHILIP BENHAM

Platform 2 at Whitby, built for exclusive use by North Yorkshire Moors Railway trains. NIGEL TROTTER

CHAPTER 12

FROM MOORS TO COAST
The route described

LNER apple green on a set of Gresley teak coaches on an LNER line! Visiting B1 4-6-0 No. 61306 *Mayflower*, one of two members of the Thompson class to survive, heads through Eller Beck. BRIAN SHARPE

To say that stunning upland scenery has been pivotal to the success of the North Yorkshire Moors Railway is a gross understatement.

The appeal of the moorland journey, which is magnificent at all times of the year, and the seaside destination of Whitby makes the heritage railway a double attraction in one.

It is a classic case of the 'best' part of a closed route having been reopened as a heritage line. South of Pickering, the closed six mile stretch to Rillington Junction is largely flat and lacks the 'wow' factor of the 18 miles to the north.

Even if the main road to the immediate south of Pickering station and other buildings on the old formation did not present a major obstacle, there would be little commercial incentive for a line which is now primarily a tourist attraction based around stunning landscapes to raise vast sums of money in extending south, apart from providing another route for incoming charters.

Another route where the most visually attractive sections have been given a second lease of life are the GWR Ruabon to Dolgellau route in mid-Wales, where the mountain section through the Dee Valley is now the Llangollen Railway, while the stretch which runs along the south shore of Llyn Tegid is the Bala Lake Railway.

Then there is the Midland & Great Northern Joint Railway system all but closed in 1959. If there was a closed section to cherrypick for reopening, it had to be what is now the North Norfolk Railway between Sheringham and Holt, with its unique combination of coastal scenery, the pine tree belt, purple-clad heathland and rolling pastures inland.

It is easily argued that one of the finest ways to see landscape typical of the North York Moors National Park is from the elevated heights of a 25mph steam train. No traffic congestion, changeable weather not a problem, no driving round searching for car parks, and the ability to get off at each station and walk through remote moorland scenery to unspoiled stone villages, cafes and pubs. Indeed, it is possible to base a week's holiday using the line as public transport, for it can offer something different to see and do every day.

Out of season is also a splendid time to enjoy the line. The glorious golden hues and changing colours of autumn amid the stunning heathlands and valleys make for some of the finest railway photography to be had anywhere.

Experienced lensmen favour mid-autumn, when the oak and birch trees of the Esk Valley are clothed in golden hues of autumn foliage, and the moorland around Goathland is carpeted in rich brown bracken.

After the train leaves Pickering station, it slows down for the level crossings at High Mill and Trout Farm, and enters the national park at Newbridge.

Before closure the route to Whitby was double tracked, and one day the NYMR may re-lay the second line to increase capacity, though throughout the pre-heritage era it had been single track. Drivers must carry a single line token to enter the section of the line beyond Newbridge.

On the left is the permanent way depot where vehicles for track maintenance are kept.

The route chosen by Stephenson hugs Pickering Beck up Newton Dale for the next 10 miles.

Meltwaters from a massive lake 11 miles long and 400ft deep in Eskdale carved out the valley during the last Ice Age. Since the 1920s, much of the gorge has been forested.

Beyond the reverse curves at Kingthorpe is Farwath, which has a pair of early railways cottages next to a farm. They once received drinking water by train, and on Pickering market days, services would stop to pick up goods or shoppers.

LEVISHAM STATION

Serving a moorland village a mile way, the lonely and picturesque Levisham station, seven miles north of Pickering, is served by one hill road.

It has been restored in 1912 style, and has appeared in several film and TV productions including Sherlock Holmes, Brideshead Revisited and All Creatures Great and Small.

It is a superb place to leave the train to explore the moorland. A gravel forest road runs up the valley to the next stop, Newton Dale Halt.

Skelton Tower stands on the hill overlooking the railway. It is not as old as it looks: far from being a medieval ruin, it was built in about 1850 by the Reverend Robert Skelton, vicar of Levisham.

Beyond Levisham, the line rises on gradients as steep as 1-in-49 as the sides of Newton Dale 'close in' to great dramatic effect.

NEWTON DALE HALT

Here is a rare example of a new station on a line closed by Beeching. It was opened in 1981 with help from the Countryside Commission and a NER-style wooden shelter was opened in 2004, broadly based on the design of the one which used to stand at Sledmere & Fimber on the closed Malton & Driffield Railway.

It is said that the halt is further from a public road than any other in England. It is designed for hill walkers, and offers four different waymarked walks. One runs to Newton Dale Well, which is to be found at the foot of Killing Nab.

This was once a popular destination for visitors who came to the natural spa waters. Plans were drawn up to develop Newton Dale into a full-sized spa town like Buxton, Cheltenham or Tunbridge wells, but thankfully they never took off and left this piece of moorland magic untroubled.

New-build A1 Pacific No. 60163 *Tornado* heads the teak 'Flying Scotsman' into Levisham during a visit to the line. BRIAN SHARPE

A stranger in LNER territory, London Brighton & South Coast Railway 'Terrier' 0-6-0T No. 36278, also known as *Knowle*, visited the NYMR from its Kent & East Sussex Railway home in October 2003. BRIAN SHARPE

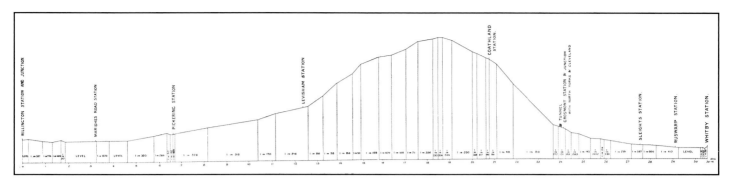

FEN BOG

Beyond a set of tight curves, the track straightens out and leaves the 20th century afforestation behind.

It then climbs steadily through Northdale to reach the 40ft deep Fen Bog. As stated earlier, Stephenson used the method he employed to take the Liverpool & Manchester Railway across Chat Moss by floating the track on a raft, here made from wattle fences resting on heather-stuffed fleeces.

It is a truly flexible solution, for the water level of the bog rises in wet weather and the railway line adjusts accordingly.

Fen Bog is a nature reserve with a unique mixture of bird species, dragonflies, wild flowers and remnants of the birch, alder and willow forest that grew here 10,000 years ago.

The northern edge of the bog marks the highest point of the railway, 532ft above sea level.

Right: LMS 'Black Five' No. 45428 waits with its train at Grosmont in June 2013. ROBIN JONES

Lambton, Hetton & Joicey Colliery Railway tank No. 29 crosses Bridge 31 during the 2014 spring steam gala. PHILIP BENHAM

Yes, it really does snow in Aidensfield! A seasonal setting at Goathland station proved a big draw despite plummeting temperatures. BRIAN SHARPE

A footpath from Beck Hole village follows the line adjacent to Eller Beck towards Thomason Foss, where visiting LNER K4 2-6-0 No. 61994 *The Great Marquess* is captured in action. BRIAN SHARPE

Few positions for taking silhouettes exist on the line. The easiest of them to reach is at Moorgates, where the line runs on an embankment before passing over the Eller Beck road, and where 1918-built NER Q6 0-8-0 No. 63395 is seen heading a freight charter against a cloud-mottled sky. BRIAN SHARPE

THE BYPASS ROUTE

The heritage railway splits from Stephenson's original formation of 1836 near milepost 19½. The old track crossed a cattle arch which allowed the movement of animals beneath. Two gatehouses here are known as Moorgates and were built to house railway staff.

Moorgates is the only place on the heritage line where a public road passes under the line, and is a highly prized location for photographers.

The present line crosses Eller Beck three times before it passes beneath Barnet House Bridge to enter the classic setting of Goathland station, which opened on July 1, 1865. A favourite of visitors to the moors, it is internationally famous as 'Aidensfield' in the ITV series Heartbeat.

Goathland was the last of the steam era stations to be built on the line, and still retains its original hand-operated crane. Its goods shed is now a popular tea room.

In 1986, Scarborough Borough Council installed the North Eastern Railway footbridge from Howdon-on-Tyne.

The small wooden signalbox which stood north of the level crossing at Marishes Road station on the lost Pickering to Rillington Junction section is now used here as a store.

A 3½ mile rail trail from Goathland follows the route of Stephenson's original line and its incline.

DOWN TO GROSMONT

Beyond Goathland, the line drops at 1-in-49 for nearly three miles, through wooded cuttings and past fields of sheep bounded by centuries-old stone walls. For steam locomotive lovers, such sections are the essence of what the NYMR is all about, with main line locomotives spectacularly storming up one of the steepest railway gradients in Britain.

The railway enters a cutting named Mill Scar which was infamously unstable for a long time, with rockfalls a regular occurrence. A watchman walked the line each morning before the arrival of the mail train from York.

At Darnholm, the line curves to the west before crossing Eller Beck three times.

B1 4-6-0 No. 61264 heads through the glacial landscape of Newton Dale. BRIAN SHARPE

Bridge 30 was the focus of a major replacement scheme over the winter of 2009-10, one of the biggest ever undertaken in the history of the line, when the life-expired 145-year-old structure was replaced by a new one with an 80ft span. Despite the extreme winter weather, the project was completed to schedule with the first train running over it on March 26, 2010. On the left are the cottages at Beck Hole, the surviving remnant from a once far bigger iron ore mining community of the mid-19th century.

The North Eastern Railway dug a new cutting for the railway and replaced a farm that lay in its path. Once out of the cutting, the railway runs 100ft above the valley floor.

Half a mile further on, the line crosses the Murk Esk on the Esk Valley viaduct. An embankment at right angles to the line once carried a narrow gauge railway from a whinstone quarry.

Until recently, the hamlet of Esk Valley could be reached only by rail. It was built to house workers at an ironstone mine which operated from 1860 to 1876.

Just before Grosmont, the railway rejoins Stephenson's route and the rail trail.

GROSMONT STATION

Entered through a tunnel alongside Stephenson's original, Grosmont is the northern terminus of the NYMR proper and has been restored as it would have been under British Railways in 1952, and lies at the heart of a thriving village.

It is also the site for the NYMR's locomotive sheds and workshops.

Visiting LNER Pacific A4 No. 4464 *Bittern* passes Esk Valley with a 9.28am Grosmont-Pickering service in May 2014. PHILIP BENHAM

LNER pair K4 No. 61994 *The Great Marquess* and K1 No. 62005 pass beneath the stupendous Larpool viaduct as they double head out of Whitby. BRIAN SHARPE

B1 4-6-0 No. 61264 (as No. 61034 *Chiru*) approaches Darnholm on a Matt Fisher photo charter. PHILIP BENHAM

Esk Valley cottages occupy the foreground as visiting GWR 0-6-0T No. 6619 heads a freight charter tender first.

Gresley A4 No. 4464 *Bittern* – which in 2013 set a new heritage-era steam speed record of 93mph on the main line – passes Water Ark with an 11.37am Grosmont-Pickering service in May 2014. PHILIP BENHAM

RAMBLES ON THE YORKSHIRE COAST AND MOORS
By **JOHN HORNBY** Price Sixpence
LONDON AND NORTH EASTERN RAILWAY

LNER guide to rambles over the North Yorkshire Moors and coast including walks from stations between Whitby and Pickering. ROBIN JONES COLLECTION

LNER B1 No. 61264 (masquerading as No. 61034 *Chiru*) passes Green End during a Matt Fisher photo charter during the line's 2014 spring steam gala. PHILIP BENHAM

THE GLORIOUS GOLDEN HUES AND CHANGING COLOURS OF AUTUMN AMID THE STUNNING HEATHLANDS AND VALLEYS MAKE FOR SOME OF THE FINEST RAILWAY PHOTOGRAPHY TO BE HAD ANYWHERE.

Many of the station buildings date from 1845 when the horse-drawn railway was converted to steam. Grosmont was then appropriately called Tunnel with its public house the Tunnel Inn. The station was enlarged again with the opening of the Esk Valley line to Battersby and Stockton-on-Tees in 1865.

Today trains on both lines stop at Grosmont, and the NYMR station now boasts four platforms. Enlarged in the heritage era, the station has lamp posts and flower tubs that came from closed stations between Hull and Scarborough, a booking office from nearby Sleights and a footbridge crossing the Esk Valley line from Robertsbridge in East Sussex. In 1996, a new signalbox, Grosmont Crossing, was opened, with the 52-lever frame from Horden, near Hartlepool.

Unusually, it has two gate wheels, which are necessary to open and close the crossing gates, which are twice as wide as the road.

A footpath leads through Stephenson's tunnel to the locomotive sheds and workshop, which has a viewing gallery and shop.

The mechanical coal hopper, designed and built by NYMR staff for refilling locomotive tenders was the first to be built in Britain since the Fifties. It eradicated the need for revivalists to shovel coal by hand from lorries at the nearby level crossing.

Grosmont is an ideal starting place for a day's photography with its main line connection and for those arriving by car, it has a sizeable pay-and-display car park close to the station.

MAIN LINE TO WHITBY

Beyond Grosmont, the NYMR joins the Esk Valley line and therefore the national rail network.

The scenery changes from moorland to open valley pastures alongside the River Esk, which is bridged by the railway nine times before Whitby is reached 6¼ miles to the east.

At Sleights, the driver stops to telephone the signalman at Nunthorpe for permission to proceed.

The next station is Ruswarp, which dates from 1847. Beyond there, the Esk becomes tidal. One of its curves was cut out to build the railway. Very soon, the spectacular 915ft long Larpool viaduct swings into view as the track curves beneath it.

Designed by architect C A Rowlandson of Charles Fox & Sons, to carry the Middlesbrough to Scarborough railway over the valley of the Esk, work on building it began on October 17, 1882. The first locomotive crossed it on October 31, 1884.

Supported on 12 piers, three of which are built on a twist to avoid deflecting the course of the tidal river, it stands 125ft above the river bed and cost £40,000 to build. It is of literary interest as it was mentioned in Bram Stoker's novel Dracula.

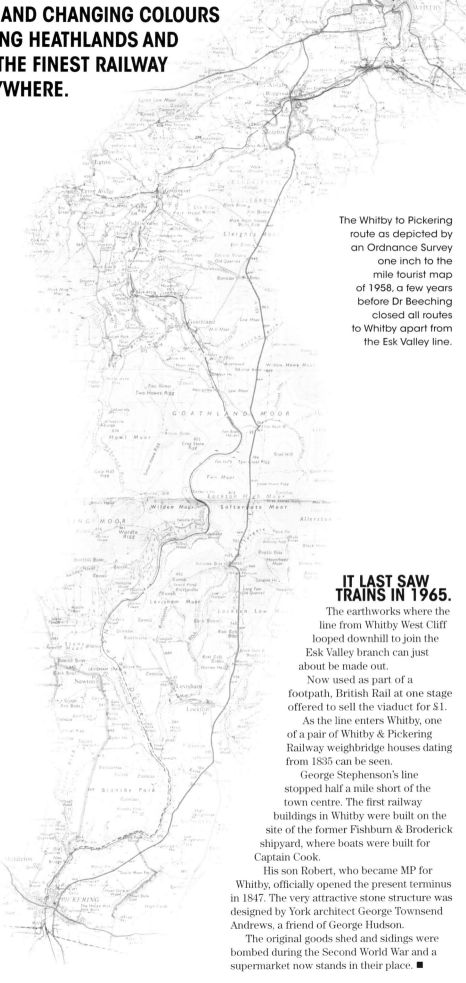

The Whitby to Pickering route as depicted by an Ordnance Survey one inch to the mile tourist map of 1958, a few years before Dr Beeching closed all routes to Whitby apart from the Esk Valley line.

IT LAST SAW TRAINS IN 1965.

The earthworks where the line from Whitby West Cliff looped downhill to join the Esk Valley branch can just about be made out.

Now used as part of a footpath, British Rail at one stage offered to sell the viaduct for £1.

As the line enters Whitby, one of a pair of Whitby & Pickering Railway weighbridge houses dating from 1835 can be seen.

George Stephenson's line stopped half a mile short of the town centre. The first railway buildings in Whitby were built on the site of the former Fishburn & Broderick shipyard, where boats were built for Captain Cook.

His son Robert, who became MP for Whitby, officially opened the present terminus in 1847. The very attractive stone structure was designed by York architect George Townsend Andrews, a friend of George Hudson.

The original goods shed and sidings were bombed during the Second World War and a supermarket now stands in their place. ∎

CHAPTER 13

RE-RAISING THE ROOF

The original Pickering trainshed roof prior to its removal by British Railways. NYMR COLLECTION

One of the finest achievements of the North Yorkshire Moors Railway has been the re-creation of Pickering station's original roof, turning it into one of the flagship termini in the heritage sector.

The station was opened by the York & North Midland Railway in 1847 to the design of architect George Townsend Andrews.

It included a covered trainshed to a 'Euston truss design' following the principles used for that station by the London & Birmingham Railway.

In 1952, after more than a century's use, British Railways removed the corroded trainshed roof to save on maintenance and renewal costs, replacing it with functional platform canopies.

This was the condition in which NYMR took over the station in 1975, but from the start it was a cherished ambition to restore the station to its former glory.

The old canopies are taken down. PHILIP BENHAM

Above: BR Standard 4MT 2-6-0 No. 76079 enters under the new trainshed roof at Pickering with the 2pm from Whitby on April 1, 2011. PHILIP BENHAM

The new roof under construction. PHILIP BENHAM

Phase 1, started in the late 1990s, saw the Heritage Lottery Fund helping to pay for major restoration work to the main station buildings, and was officially opened by Prince Charles on October 2, 2010, with Phase 2 taking place in 2010/11. This work under the title Train of Thought, reflecting the educational aspect of the project, included a new Learning Centre (with conference facilities and climate controlled archive) and Visitor Centre, built by York contractor WM Birch, and opening in 2010. The project continued over the 2010-11 winter with the trainshed roof reconstructed by building contractor Houltons of Hull.

Faithfully following the original Andrews design, careful research was carried out to make sure every detail was as accurate as possible, including the colour scheme, while ensuring modern building standards and regulations were complied with.

The work was completed in time for the 2011 main season despite the contractors battling against some of the heaviest snowfall in decades throughout December and January, with the first train passing under the new roof on April 1, 2011. The replacement roof cost a total of £556,000 and provides additional support to the fabric of the 19th century station buildings.

Overall the scheme cost £1.25 million with the majority of the funding coming from the Heritage Lottery Fund and the former Yorkshire Forward – together with a smaller grant for the Learning Centre from Yorwaste.

On May 9, 2013, the railway unveiled a plaque for the National Railway Heritage Awards' Ian Allan Publishing Award for the Train of Thought project. The award was won by the heritage line against extremely stiff competition such as the refurbishment of London's St Pancras Hotel and the repainting of the Forth Bridge.

The Learning Centre was named after NYMR's long-time archivist Graham Reussner. ■

The WH Smith newsagent's kiosk which was in position at the station in NER days has been re-created. ROBIN JONES

CHAPTER 14

BRIDGE OF ICE

Are our heritage railways ticking time bombs? Much work and money goes on maintaining the vital infrastructure on which the safe operation of the railways depend.

Many of Britain's preserved lines are built on routes which date back to Victorian times. Inevitably there will come the day when structures such as earthworks, bridges and tunnels will need expensive maintenance and repairs, often unexpected and way beyond annual budget allocations. In this century, both the Severn Valley and Gloucestershire Warwickshire railways suffered cataclysmic flooding, the latter because the Great Western Railway was found to have laid an embankment directly on flat ground without installing proper drainage.

On the North Yorkshire Moors Railway, the iron skew Bridge 30 is one of those on the deviation line built by the North Eastern Railway and opened in 1865.

It was strengthened in 1906 and again in 1908, but otherwise remained largely unaltered into the preservation era, but problems began stacking up.

By early this century, the bridge was showing serious signs of deterioration and after many years of careful monitoring the decision was made to replace it. If it had remained in place, severe weight restrictions would have had to be imposed, making it impossible for anything bigger than a tank engine to operate, and this in turn would have threatened the whole future of the NYMR.

It was never going to be an easy project but the task was made more difficult by the bridge's location deep in the Eller Beck gorge at Water Ark between Goathland and Grosmont, with limited road access only possible alongside the track.

After careful evaluation, it was decided to retain the original abutments but to replace the iron bridge decking and girders with a new steel composite construction, consisting of two plate girders with precast concrete decking incorporating cantilever walkways and open steel parapets.

The design was worked up by Cass Hayward LLP and the main girders manufactured by Mabey Bridge – both of Chepstow.

Construction Marine Ltd of Leeds was appointed as principal contractor. In parallel with the design and preparation was the all-important issue of funding, as the high cost of such a major project was beyond the normal means of the NYMR.

A £1 million Bridges & Wheels Appeal fundraising campaign was launched, including on-train collections by NYMR volunteers, a gala fundraising ball at the National Railway Museum, a series of limited edition prints by NYMR artist in residence Christopher Ware, and a series of road shows. The 'wheels' part of the appeal was aimed at restoring BR Standard 4MT 2-6-4T No. 80135.

More than £300,000 was raised from these initiatives. The balance was made up by grants from North Yorkshire County Council and the Rural Development Programme for England (RDPE).

As luck would have it, NYMR and its contractors found they had chosen the worst winter weather for 20 years to begin the work, which began in earnest in early January 2010, but the contractors were hampered by heavy

In February 2005, NYMR officials using the line's inspection saloon assess the deterioration of Bridge 30. PHILIP BENHAM

Above: Southern Railway Schools 4-4-0 No. 30926 *Repton* heads 'The Moorlander' dining train over Bridge 30 on March 27, 2010. BRIAN SHARPE

Bridge 30 before replacement: the line's flagship, A4 Pacific No. 60007 *Sir Nigel Gresley*, heads the 'Flying Scotsman' over it. PHILIP BENHAM

snow which made the remote site very difficult to access.

However, helped by the generous loan by rail contractor VolkerRail of a high-capacity Kirow crane, the old girders were removed and a new beam installed, having been brought down the Esk Valley line by rail from A V Dawson's yard in Middlesbrough on January 4. The availability of the crane saved having to steam the NYMR's two steam breakdown cranes for what would have been a very difficult job.

The lifting out of the old beams had been scheduled to take place between January 4-11; however, a combination of poor weather and the discovery that what had been thought to be steel girders were made of wrought iron, making them much harder to cut, slowed progress to the point where it was running several days late.

This caused a major problem as there was a limited window before the Kirow crane was due to return to its more usual duties on the national network on February 15. Fortunately there was some slippage built into the

The removal of the old girders in January 2010. PHILIP BENHAM

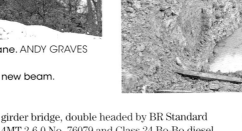

Above: Bridge 30 being lifted out by the Kirow crane. ANDY GRAVES

Right: The digging out of the abutments ready for a new beam.
PHILIP BENHAM

programme, so it was possible to gain some time through weekend working, albeit at extra cost.

With the old girders removed, work began on modifying the abutments so as to be able to cast new concrete bearers for the new beams, this being a rate-limiting step as the concrete needed to cure to sufficient strength to bear the weight of the crane and bridge beams.

The first of three concrete pours was made just three days after the beams had been lifted out, on January 22. Fortunately, by modifying the concrete mix and using heaters, the required strength was reached quite quickly. In the event the first beam was not lifted out until January 14, and it was to take a further five days before the remaining pieces were removed, the whole structure having proved to be very well fastened together.

While all this was taking place, the NYMR's permanent way group had another problem to contend with if delivery of the concrete decking sections was not to be hindered. These would be delivered by road to Newbridge Yard, Pickering, then moved by train to the work site, but a landslip at Bridge 18 in Newtondale caused by the heavy snow had undermined the track there, making it unsafe to use.

The bank therefore had to be dug out so that stone-filled gabion baskets could be placed to reinforce the bank over a length of around 45 yards and to a depth of 11 feet. This work was completed over the course of two weeks.

Once the new bridge beams had been lifted into place, the masonry around the new concrete bearers had to be rebuilt and then the 26 concrete decking sections, each weighing around six tonnes, were lifted into place.

In the meantime, NYMR services operated on weekends between Grosmont and Goathland, also on the Esk Valley line between Grosmont and Whitby as well as Grosmont and Battersby. The trains were well patronised despite the poor weather, again underlining the vision of those who pushed for the extension of services from the heritage line over Network Rail metals to Whitby.

Finally, ballast was laid and the track reinstated in time for the new season. So, despite the weather, the work was completed on time and to budget ready for the first train to cross on Saturday, March 27, 2010. Soon after 9am, the first passenger train to cross the superb new £750,000 concrete-decked steel girder bridge, double headed by BR Standard 4MT 2-6-0 No. 76079 and Class 24 Bo-Bo diesel electric D5061, broke through a banner to celebrate the occasion.

On board the crowded train, passengers who had each paid a £5 supplement to be the first across the new structure, and would each receive a commemoration certificate, pressed their faces to carriage windows to catch a glimpse of the newly opened view of the tumbling beck below, previously hidden by the girders of the old bridge.

There was a carnival atmosphere all weekend, with a full timetable of trains and special £10 shuttle services between Goathland and the new bridge utilising the sumptuous Great Western saloon. Refreshments were served on board, and each shuttle stopped on Bridge 30 so that passengers could alight and walk along the concrete footway to examine the new structure at close quarters.

During the short journeys, the railway's civil engineer Nigel Trotter was on hand to describe the history of the old bridge and the engineering details of the new one – but the service was interrupted after D5061 failed on Saturday's second shuttle and was rescued by SR Schools 4-4-0 No 30926 *Repton*, that had just brought in a train from Whitby to Grosmont.

Nigel said that even during his BR days he had never experienced such terrible weather conditions as the construction workers had when they doggedly battled to finish the work on time.

Other motive power in use on the Saturday were SR S15 4-6-0 No. 825, LNWR Super D 0-8-0 No. 49395 as well as the railway's first generation DMU.

The appeal turned out to be an outstanding success, and even during the grand bridge reopening weekend, staff lost no opportunity to ask for more money as they went through the trains. Even the scrap metal from the old bridge raised £19,150 towards the appeal.

A few weeks later on Monday, April 19, the bridge was officially opened by Pete Waterman, who had been patron of the Bridge 30 Appeal, at a ceremony in which the bridge was blessed by the Bishop of Whitby.

The preservation movement has completed many 'missions impossible' but few in conditions as severe at this. ■

The first train headed by BR Standard 4MT 2-6-0 No. 76079 and Class 24 Bo-Bo diesel electric D5061 breaks through a banner to mark the completion of one of the most gruelling projects in the history of the preservation movement. PHILIP BENHAM

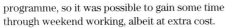

Above: Two days to go before the scheduled reopening on March 27, 2010, and new track is in place. PHILIP BENHAM

Left: The steel span was lifted into place on February 14, 2010, with work on the concrete decking begun. BRIAN SHARPE

CHAPTER 15

GREAT GALA GUESTS

In so many ways, the North Yorkshire Moors Railway was fortunate in being able to operate the whole of its line from the date of opening on May 1, 1973.

In the case of other heritage railways, they have started with a few lengths of track, or even no track at all, taking years to reach the next goal and the one after that, and many marvellous achievements have been accomplished in the process.

However, having all 18 miles from Grosmont to Pickering available from the start, rather than having to relay parts of it as time and funds allowed, gave the NYMR a head start.

Almost from the outset, the 'starter line' mantle of small industrial saddle tanks hauling one or two coaches was discarded, and big main line locomotives became the order of the day. It was a huge foundation on which to build success.

Annual audited figures for UK heritage railways stated that in 2012, there were 10.3 million visitors, with 7.1 million passengers giving employment to 2000 employees supported by 17,000 volunteers. This success produced a turnover of £92 million and contributed £250 million to local economies.

Thanks to volunteers across the country,

just like those who saved the Grosmont to Pickering line back in the late Sixties, today's heritage railway industry is an established, thriving and growing entity.

It has been calculated that only around 5% of passengers on many heritage railways are hardcore enthusiasts, with the remaining 95% ordinary families. Studies elsewhere have conjectured that for every pound spent on a steam railway, three more pounds are spent in the local economy.

The great railway magnate George Hudson, who invested heavily in turning Whitby into a mainstream holiday resort in the mid-19th century, would therefore have loved the NYMR.

As a major attraction in the national park, it ensures a steady stream of tourists, but not as he envisaged back then, arriving by rail, but travelling there because of the railway!

One major way in which heritage railways benefit holiday regions is their ability to extend the season.

Traditionally Easter, the spring bank holiday week and late July to early September, heritage lines are an all-round attraction, of interest in all weathers. Of special note here are galas and other special events, which fill up hotels, guest houses and restaurants on

weekends out of season which two decades or more ago, local traders would have written off.

The NYMR's spring and autumn galas each year are now a major part of the enthusiast calendar, not to mention the immensely-popular wartime weekend, as described in the next chapter.

The spring gala is usually held in late April or early May, and the autumn gala at the end of September or early October.

The enthusiast fraternity eagerly awaits announcements on which locomotives have been hired in as guests for the big events, and work out the photographic possibilities that each affords, with particular engine and coaching stock combinations running through the stunning landscapes and the many vistas that unfold at different times of the year.

Highly prized are scenes of LNER locomotives hauling rakes of teak stock, restored to perfection at Pickering over several decades by the sterling efforts of the LNER Coach Association, a leader in its field.

Many big-name locomotives have run on the NYMR over the past four decades, and here are views of many of them in action in this unique and wonderful moorland landscape that draws visitors back time and time again.

Unique BR 8P Pacific No. 71000 *Duke of Gloucester* leaves Goathland for Pickering on September 26 during the 2008 autumn steam gala. BRIAN SHARPE

In April 2005, the NYMR held a Gresley 100 gala over three weekends, to mark the centenary of Nigel Gresley's appointment as Great Northern Railway carriage and wagon superintendent. Held in conjunction with the LNER Coach Association, the gala was different in that it placed as much emphasis on coaching stock as on locomotives. A £48,500 Heritage Lottery Fund grant allowed teak coaches to visit from other lines such as the Seven Valley, Bo'ness & Kinneil, Bluebell and Embsay & Bolton Abbey Steam railways. Visiting LNER V2 2-8-2 No. 60800 *Green Arrow* is seen heading the 9.45am from Grosmont past Esk Valley on April 17. BRIAN SHARPE

The last word in British Rail steam: passing Water Ark on October 1 during the 2005 autumn steam gala are 'Black Fives' No. 45110, which hauled the last BR steam train on all, the 1T57 'Fifteen Guinea Special' on August 11, 1968, and No. 45212, which hauled the last scheduled steam train the week before. It was the first heritage era pairing of these two. BRIAN SHARPE

B1 4-6-0 No. 1306 *Mayflower* passes Thomason Foss on May 5, 2013.

GWR 4-4-0 No. 3440 *City of Truro,* which in 1904 set an unofficial world steam speed record of 102.3mph, being the first to claimed to have broken the 100mph barrier, is helped by GWR 0-6-2T No. 6619 up the 1-in-49 gradient past Beck Hole on April 29, 2006. STEVE ARMITAGE

Aboove left: One of the star guests at the 2009 autumn steam gala was BR Britannia Pacific No. 70013 *Oliver Cromwell,* seen rounding the curve on the approach to Levisham station, with Q6 0-8-0 No. 63395 waiting with a demonstration freight working. JOHN HUGHES

Above: LNWR 'Super D' 0-8-0 No. 49395, part of the National Collection, heads an engineers' train up the gradient at Green End on September 30, 2006. DAVE RODGERS

When the planned Rail 2000 Millennium Cavalcade of Steam at Shildon marking the 175th anniversary of the Stockton & Darlington Railway was cancelled seven weeks before it was due to take place, the NYMR stepped in and arranged a replacement but slimmed-down event under the banner of Rail 175 during October 6-8 that year. Among the guests was Furness Railway A5 0-4-0 No. 20 which, built in 1863, is Britain's oldest operational standard gauge locomotive. It is seen approaching Pickering. ROBIN JONES

The October 1-3 autumn steam gala in 2010 was organised with a Somerset & Dorset Joint Railway theme. In what could have been a typical scene from the latter years of the legendary trans-Mendip route, SDJR 7F 2-8-0 No. 53809 pilots visiting Bulleid Battle of Britain light Pacific No. 34070 *Manston* up the 1-in-49 gradients at Esk Valley. DAVE RODGERS

Llangollen Railway flagship Western Region 4-6-0 No. 7822 *Foxcote Manor* climbs past Water Ark on October 2 during the 2011 autumn steam gala. KARL HEATH

Repainted into the 'enthusiasts' choice' of British Railways Brunswick green, new-build A1 Peppercorn Pacific No. 60163 *Tornado* travelled to the NYMR under its own steam via the Esk Valley line for a 10 day gala in spring 2009. It is seen rounding the curve at Darnholm with the 9.30am Grosmont to Pickering service on May 2. BRIAN SHARPE

Great Central Railway-based Great Northern Railway N2 0-6-2T leaves Grosmont for Pickering during the 2012 autumn steam gala. BRIAN SHARPE

Below: Visiting from the Churnet Valley Railway, USATC S160 2-8-0 No. 6046 passes the Deviation Junction footpath during the 2013 autumn steam gala. PHILIP BENHAM

LNER K4 2-6-0 No. 61994 *The Great Marquess*, which hauled the last special train from Whitby to Scarborough and Malton in March 2005 with K1 No. 62005, returned to the NYMR for the September 28-30, 2007 autumn steam gala. It passes Moorgates on the climb from Goathland with the LNER Coach Association's teak set. BRIAN SHARPE

Visiting GNR 0-6-2T No. 1744 heads through Northdale on May 22, 2010. PHILIP BENHAM

Class 5 power: Ian Riley's visiting LMS 'Black Five' No. 45407 and B1 No. 61264 as No. 61034 *Chiru* at Goathland during the 2014 spring gala. PHILIP BENHAM

Left: LNER 4-6-0 No. 61306 *Mayflower* climbs through Beck Hole with an afternoon Pickering train on May 11, 2013. MAURICE BURNS

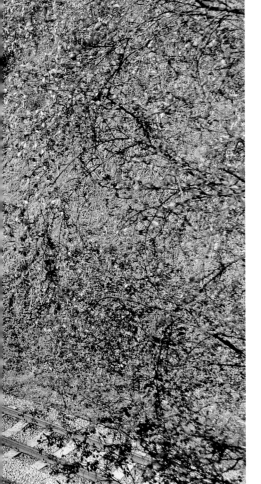

During a brief visit to the 2014 spring gala, Great Central Railway-based LMS 'Jinty' 3F 0-6-0T No. 47406 hauls a short freight at Beck Hole. PHILIP BENHAM

CHAPTER 16

RAF airmen off duty between bombing raids over the continent. TIM DURRANT

THE MOORS AT WAR!

Forever linked in the public's mind with TV show Heartbeat, one of the most popular events on the North Yorkshire Moors Railway recreates an era two decades before the 'Swinging Sixties'.

For three days every autumn, the clock is turned back to the Second World War. The peak summer period having ended, hundreds of wartime re-enactors populate the trains and stations, dressed as servicemen and women, factory workers, land army girls, nurses, air raid wardens, black marketeers and all the other characters that you would expect to find on the streets of Yorkshire during the conflict.

Thousands of people travel from far and wide to see the event for themselves, often donning period costume to join in.

The Wartime Weekend is an annual tribute to the men and women who kept Britain's railways running through the war, and has an international reputation for authenticity.

The weekend begins with the ceremonial flag raising on Friday when the clock is put back to 1943, and continues until it is lowered again on Sunday afternoon.

All the stations from Grosmont to Pickering are dressed with wartime notices, sandbags and blacked-out windows. On the Saturday, there is a parade through Pickering, with the High Street area sealed off as the town becomes a huge showcase for everyday life in the Forties.

The appearance of wartime German uniforms is always a sensitive issue but as the railway is open to all, it would be difficult stop entirely. So the decision was made a few years ago for Levisham station to take on the guise of a French village, Le Visham, and to spend the entire event under German occupation.

Le Visham has subsequently become a popular attraction during the event.

A German paratrooper unit may re-enact a training drop from a mock up glider, in a field behind the German camp site, and on occasion a V1 doodlebug rocket demonstration was held in the forest beside the track (contrary to popular belief at the time, it was not targeted at the general manager's office in Pickering). On Le Visham station, a French beer tent called Café Allée de Bois serves French fare, with accordion music playing. At one recent event, the real Herr Flick – actor Richard Gibson – and Helga, played by Kim Hartman, from the BBC TV series 'Allo 'Allo! put in an appearance.

In Goathland the station is usually looked after by the Home Guard, while all the shops have windows taped up and Union Flag bunting draped over the shop fronts. The tea

In the service of their country.
DISCOVERYORKSHIRECOAST.COM

Is your journey really necessary? Waiting for the train. NYMR

Soldiers on patrol at Goathland. NYMR

A German soldier checking a carriage at Le Visham. NYMR

Lovely spam, wonderful spam!
DISCOVERYORKSHIRECOAST.COM

The wartime canteen. JULIE COWDY/KIRKBYMOORSIDE CLUB

Sandbags protect this guards' post on Goathland station's platform. NYMR

An army jeep parked in Pickering High Street.
NYMR

An army officer dances with a local girl on the platform at Grosmont.
JULIE COWDY/KIRKBYMOORSIDE CLUB

"Don't panic Mr Mainwaring!" A Home Guard member on duty at Goathland. NYMR

"We'll meet again…"
DISCOVERYORKSHIRECOAST.COM

rooms even have a wartime menu. At Pickering there are re-enactments, including the occasional air raid ably dealt with by the ARPS and Red Cross staff. Other events might include a cookery demonstration of typical wartime produce. A key element throughout is the musical entertainment with numbers performed by singers and comedians – often courtesy of the Forces' entertainment unit, ENSA, helped down by copious cups of tea from the NAAFI hut on platform 2.

The origin of the event dates to the 1990s when NYMR shops manager Alan Smith – who had a keen interest in the RAF and Royal Observer Corps, plus contacts at Eden Camp and the Yorkshire Air Museum – approached the line's former chief executive Ken Kitching with the idea. Costumes were found, displays organised and the event grew steadily.

But it really took off after the Reverend Ivon Baker became involved in 1996. Over the years Ivon, who died in 2011, moulded it into NYMR's most popular special event.

The NYMR has now expanded the event to the Pickering showground, providing park and ride facilities and even more re-enactments. ∎

Whacko! A schoolmaster of the Forties.
JULIE COWDY/KIRKBYMOORSIDE CLUB

Wartime paper sellers on duty outside Pickering station. NYMR

Platform reunion time. DISCOVERYORKSHIRECOAST.COM

Crowds line the platform at Pickering. NYMR

A German radio transmitting station. NYMR

Fashion in an age of austerity. DISCOVERYORKSHIRECOAST.COM

US Army personnel await to board a train. DISCOVERYORKSHIRECOAST.COM

CHAPTER 17

What about a
SOUTHERN EXTENSION?

Since the North Yorkshire Moors Railway became established, the question has been frequently asked – what about rebuilding the missing 6½ miles running south from Pickering to the main line at Rillington Junction?

Indeed, for many reasons it seems an excellent idea, not least of all because there would be the potential of through passengers from York, Leeds and beyond to the heritage line from the south. Reconnecting any sizeable town to the national network and restoring services is always a good idea, if only in terms of social benefits. However, as proponents have pointed out in the past, there is the prospect of a 56 mile steam highway between the National Railway Museum in York, arguably the best of its kind in the world, and Whitby via Pickering.

For those enthusiasts who study old Ordnance Survey maps and postulate about the possibilities of reopening a particular closed line, Rillington Junction to Pickering is a no-brainer, especially as it crosses flat terrain throughout its length.

However, the reality is very different.

Most obviously, the Bridge Street and Hungate level crossings to the immediate south of Pickering station are gone, lost when British Rail lifted the track after the revivalists took the view that Pickering was possibly too big an ask, let alone further. Beyond the site of the Hungate crossing, which takes a busy main road across the route, an Aldi supermarket now stands. No matter – if you can plan to build HS2, such obstacles are but a trifle, and in this case, the rail corridor appears to have been protected. However, the biggest obstacle of all now rears its head: finance. Even the most successful heritage railway could probably not afford the expense of reinstating this section by itself.

Beyond Pickering station, there were seven level crossings, including the immediate problem of crossing the busy A170 at Hungate and one across the A169 at Black Bull. Not only is the trend in recent years to eliminate level crossings wherever possible, but for the heritage line to operate trains over this length, a sizeable amount of manpower would be needed for this reason alone.

What would be the gain for the NYMR if the missing link to Rillington was rebuilt? One of the line's big selling points is the upland scenery: while the rolling open countryside south to Rillington is not unattractive, neither is it particularly scenic or interesting.

The extra 13 miles on a round trip would need a fares increase, and a lengthier journey for a full round trip to Whitby of more than two hours... which could deter passengers, especially those with young children, and harm the core business. The old Rillington station was some distance from the village, and while it is near today's busy A64, and therefore a good starting point for passengers, there is nothing of interest there.

Of course, if you could extend the line back into Malton, running over a short part of Network Rail's York to Scarborough line, steam trains could terminate in a town centre. However, the cost of reinstating and signalling the junction would again be prohibitive, and well out of reach of the heritage line's budget.

The NYMR takes the view that it is a heritage attraction, and while it is capable of laying on trains for local people in times of hardship such as extreme wintry weather if the need arises, it has no aspirations to become part of the regional strategic transport infrastructure. For Pickering to have a connection directly to the national network, it would need an outside body to draw up the plans, find the money to build it and run it.

There would then be the problem of an outside train operator needing to run through to Whitby to make the new line pay. A major variation in the NYMR's Light Railway Order would be needed, permitting trains to run faster than the current maximum speed of 25mph.

Furthermore, regular outside services would in theory restrict the paths available to NYMR heritage trains, threatening the viability, and changing the character of the line we know and love today.

The NYMR has its own long-term aims to reinstate at least part of the second line on its

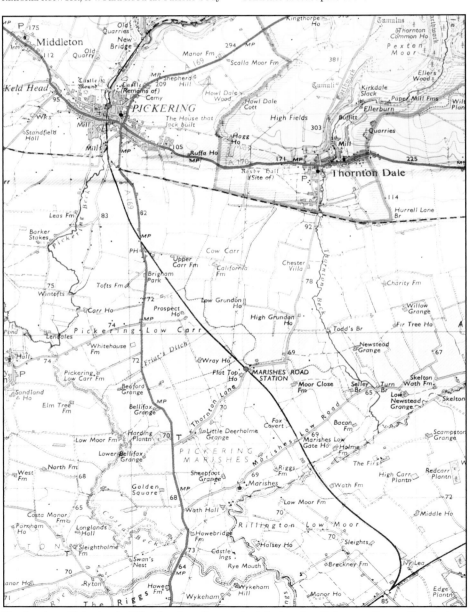

The line from Pickering to Rillington Junction as depicted on the Ordnance Survey One-Inch Map of 1958. Rillington station closed to normal passenger traffic on September 22, 1930, but was used by special trains until the 1960s. However, Marishes Road is still shown as open. The last BR train ran on July 1, 1966.

route. The section from Levisham to Goathland will be tackled first, as outlined in the strategy document Steaming On published in 2012. However, the aim would be to increase the NYMR's capacity to run more heritage trains, not to let the second line to an outside operator.

None of this is to say that a Pickering to Rillington reinstatement will never happen, but it illustrates a spacious gulf between wishful thinking and a sound and workable business plan.

NYMR general manager Philip Benham's personal view is that he would like to see the railway extended through Pickering to a car park site south of the town near Pickering Showground or the Black Bull pub which lies opposite the very short-lived Kirby station. The direct benefit there would be to alleviate passengers' parking problems in the town, but again, such a project would involve enormous cost and there are no plans for it in the foreseeable future.

Yet look at the miracles that have been achieved since Beeching's axe fell on the line – the reopening of the Whitby & Pickering Railway, the reroofing of Pickering station, the rebuilding of Bridge 30, the amassing of one of the finest heritage locomotive fleets anywhere – and then try to say that no more will ever happen.

With the NYMR attracting well over £30 million into the local economy each year, and local councillors all over Britain slowly becoming far more tuned in to the potential offered by heritage railways than they were a decade or more ago, never say never to anything. ■

Below: Kirby station opened in October 1845, named after the village of Kirby Misperton, and closed as early as October 1, 1858. The station has been occasionally referred to as Black Bull, the much nearer public house, which also gave its name to the nearby level crossing on the Pickering to Malton road. The station house, now a home, was built in stone which was unusual for minor Yorkshire & North Midland Railway stations which were more commonly built in brick, like Marishes Road. ROBIN JONES

The intermediate and isolated station of Marishes Road is today a private residence with many of its railway features preserved. It opened on July 5, 1845, and until 1848 was called High Marishes, after the nearby village. It closed to passengers on March 8, 1965, although freight to Pickering continued for a further year. The Duke of Edinburgh was probably the last passenger to alight here, when the Royal Train was stabled overnight on June 2, 1965, before visited Fylingdales early warning station the next day. ROBIN JONES

CHAPTER 18

THE NORTH RIDING'S 'OTHER' SEASIDE HERITAGE LINE

The Saltburn Cliff Lift with the classic pier in the background. ROBIN JONES

Surf's up: the cliff lift as seen from beach level. ROBIN JONES

THE North Yorkshire Moors Railway is not the only standard gauge heritage line in the locality of the national park which takes visitors to the seaside.

While the NYMR has been running as a heritage line since 1973, the Saltburn Cliff Lift has been carrying passengers since June 28, 1884.

For the price of just £1, the water-balanced funicular railway, the oldest of its type still in operation, takes holiday-makers from Marine Parade in Saltburn-by-the-Sea to the sea front, with a bottom station opposite the resort's pier which opened in 1869.

The arrival of the Stockton & Darlington Railway in Saltburn in the old North Riding of Yorkshire on August 17, 1861, marked the start of the town's career as a seaside destination.

Access to the pier from the town at the top of the steep cliff top was awkward and deterred early visitors. However, engineer John Anderson devised a solution for the Saltburn Pier Company in the form of a wooden cliff hoist. Capable of carrying 20 people in a wooden cage lowered by a rope to the beach, it opened on July 1, 1870.

In August 1883, the hoist was condemned because of its rotten timbers, and so the pier's new owner, Middlesbrough Estate, hired Sir Richard Tangye, whose company had built two water-powered funicular railways in Scarborough, to build a replacement. In turn, Tangye appointed George Croydon Marks to design one for Saltburn.

It rises 120ft using double tracks 207ft long. A pair of 12-person cars are each fitted with a 350 gallon water tank and hauled by double steel wire ropes controlled by a brakeman in the upper station.

The car at the top has its water tank filled until its mass exceeds the mass of the car at the bottom. While running down the incline, one car is counterbalanced by the mass of the other. When the car reaches the bottom, its water is released, reducing the mass of the lower car. The water is then pumped back up to the top of the cliff.

In 1924 an electrically operated water pump was installed and in 1998 the main winding wheel was replaced for the first time, while a new hydraulic braking system was installed.

Currently owned and operated by Redcar and Cleveland Borough Council, the cliff lift is open every weekend from the middle of March through to October, and daily during the peak season. ∎

View from the bottom station. ROBIN JONES

The two cars pass on the incline. ROBIN JONES